W9-BLU-682

Elizabeth

The Woman and The Queen

Elizabeth

The Woman and The Queen

Graham Turner

MACMILLAN

The Daily Telegraph

First published 2002 by Macmillan
an imprint of Pan Macmillan Ltd
Pan Macmillan, 20 New Wharf Road, London N1 9RR
Basingstoke and Oxford
Associated companies throughout the world
www.panmacmillan.com

ISBN 1 405 00030 9

1 3 5 7 9 8 6 4 2

A CIP catalogue record for this book is available from
the British Library.

Creative director: Clive Crook
Picture Research: Abi Patton
Text: Graham Turner
Typeset by SX Composing DTP, Rayleigh, Essex
Page design by Dan Newman/Perfect Bound Ltd
Printed and bound in the UK by Bath Press

Contents

Preface

This is not a biography of the Queen. There are already two perfectly good ones in existence, by Sarah Bradford and Ben Pimlott. It is, rather, a portrait of her as seen through the eyes of her family, friends and servants, scores of whom have been kind enough to talk to me at length and often with refreshing candour.

Only those who are lucky enough to be given access to the people around the Queen have any chance of understanding her real nature. Without that access, a writer has to fall back on his or her imagination and, looking back at all that has been written about the Royal Family during these last years, it is clear that monarchy is the mother of invention. I have been fortunate enough to have been granted that access for almost a decade and, since the British upper class has a tendency towards candour, have been given some very revealing insights into this extraordinary lady who, in public at least, is so pickled in formality that even a childhood friend like Lord Airlie, the former Lord Chamberlain, never calls her anything but 'Ma'am'.

For many years, I had no desire to write about members of the Royal Family, because I presumed that it would not be possible to discover the truth about their characters. Then, in 1993, I suggested to the *Daily Mail* that I might write a series of articles about the way in which Buckingham Palace worked. Little did I realize that, once one begins to write about the royal world, it is very difficult to stop, if only because those who commission articles assume that one knows a great deal more than one really does.

The Queen at Windsor Horse Trials, 1981.

As a result, I was asked by *The Daily Telegraph* to write a succession of profiles of the principal members of the Royal Family: first a seventieth birthday portrait of the Queen in 1996, followed by series about Prince Charles (1998), the Queen Mother (1999) and Prince Philip (2001).

Almost invariably, the profiles which appeared as a result caused a considerable brouhaha, partly because the material in them was both novel and candid. The number of Prince Charles's pre-marital affairs; the Queen Mother's high-spending habits and fondness for gin; the fact that the Queen and Prince Philip engage, from time to time, in what one courtier described as 'terrific mutual tongue-lashing'; the long-standing rift between Prince Philip and Prince Charles – all these became the stuff of sometimes explosive comment.

The uproar which followed the publication of extracts from this book even included suggestions that I had been trying to tarnish the Queen's Golden Jubilee and that *The Daily Telegraph*, in which they appeared, had undergone a conversion to republicanism. Nothing could have been further from the truth. The day the *Telegraph* becomes republican, the moon really will be made of green cheese! My critics were not, with a single exception, disputing the accuracy of my facts. They had their own dog-eat-dog agendas.

I wrote this book simply because I wanted to give a full and entirely candid portrait of the remarkable lady who has been our Queen for half a century. Having been given unusually detailed and poignant insights into her character, her family and her world by people close to her for many years, I would have thought it a travesty to tell less than the truths I had been shown. I do so in no malicious or carping spirit but because – given her stature and achievements – she deserves no less. Her jubilee year is surely an appropriate moment for such an assessment.

Nor are these pages full of the sort of fanciful speculation in which some royal writers are apt to indulge for lack of hard evidence. They are the product of hundreds of conversations with people who have been, and are, close to the Queen and her family.

In her public persona, Elizabeth II is one of the best-known women in the world. Hundreds of millions of words have been written about her. The files of newspapers bulge with stories about her and her family. There are shelves full of biographies of her. Her face has been appearing on stamps and the front covers of magazines since she was a child.

Yet she has remained a largely unknown woman because, believing as she does in the sacred nature of monarchy, she has kept her private self strictly apart. No nun is more dedicated. Her vows, made long before she became Queen, were as unqualified and irrevocable as the late Mother Teresa's. 'I declare before you all,' she said in her piping voice in Cape Town in 1947, 'that my whole life, whether it be long or short, shall be devoted to your service.'

From that moment, everything else – including her own family – came a poor second. She had consecrated herself to the Divine Duty of Kings, the Divine Right enjoyed by her ancient predecessors having vanished long ago.

This book is about that unknown woman and her family. It is also a portrait of her relations with the most significant members of her family – Prince Philip, Prince Charles and the late Queen Mother.

The death of the Queen Mother, so soon after the death of her sister Princess Margaret, and in the very year of her Golden Jubilee, left the Queen even more alone on the royal stage. In some ways, the Queen Mother had been her closest and most natural confidante. As a courtier said to me at the time: 'Prince Philip is always there when she needs him, but he does lead such a busy life. The Queen is often lonely.'

I remain, as I began, a monarchist, for all kinds of reasons. Apart from anything else, the alternative is too grim to contemplate: some drab, clapped-out politician who would add nothing to the gaiety of this or any other nation. Who would cross the road, still less stand for hours in the rain, to catch a glimpse of any of them? And how marvellous it is, in this age of cronydom, to have as Head of State a woman who is far above politics and needs seek the favour of no man. Surely that is what a Head of State is meant to be?

'A model of good behaviour'

1 The Young Princess

As a child, Elizabeth was almost preposterously well-behaved. Visitors to her London home in Piccadilly spoke of her 'complete serenity'. Even when she was two and a half, Winston Churchill observed in her 'an air of authority and reflectiveness astonishing in an infant'. Before she went to bed at night, she folded her clothes with military precision and was soon chiding her younger sister Margaret for what she deemed inappropriate behaviour. She was an early entrant in the paragon stakes.

She had been born in 1926 at the London home of her maternal grandparents, the Earl and Countess of Strathmore, in Bruton Street, Mayfair, the first child of the Duke and Duchess of York. Her mother was one of a large, landed but non-royal Scottish family whose principal home was Glamis Castle. Her father was the younger son of King George V. At the time, neither of Elizabeth's parents had any idea that she would one day become Queen. Her grandfather, George V, was very much alive; and her uncle, the Prince of Wales, still unmarried and a relatively young man, was expected to succeed him. This delightful little girl seemed unlikely to have to carry any of the burdens of the throne.

'It was bliss for me to have a baby like her to play with,' recalled her cousin, Lady Mary Clayton. 'She was intelligent, very imaginative and you could always get her to listen to reason. In that respect, she was utterly unlike her sister Margaret.' Another cousin, Mrs Margaret Rhodes, has the same memory of a slightly saccharine perfection. 'The Queen,' she said, 'was basically an awfully obedient, very disciplined child, goody-goody you could say. She also, in those days, did an awful lot of smiling.' Little wonder that, later, Wallis Simpson tartly nicknamed her 'Shirley Temple' after the ever-radiant American child film-star.

She also seems to have been quite an organizing little madam, in the nicest possible way, of course. 'We were endlessly playing at horses,' said Mrs Rhodes. 'We'd go out into the field at Balmoral and I'd have to be the circus horse while she, needless to say, was always the circus-master. She wasn't exactly bossy, but she was the one who initiated the games.' Elizabeth even persuaded her gruff, formidable grandfather, King George V, to get on his knees and serve as one of her steeds.

There were occasional signs of common humanity, even mild moral turpitude. 'We were playing a card game once,' said Lady Mary Clayton, 'and she cheated in order to win. My mother said, "Lilibet, you really cannot cheat!" "Oh yes, I can," she replied, "because I'm a princess." Mother said, "Very well, we'll all cheat" – so we did and, of course, the game came to an end, because it didn't work.' Other than that, there was little more than a quickly curbed flash of temper and moments of mild disobedience, but nothing, then or later, that could be called rebellion. So far as Elizabeth was concerned, traces were for staying within, not for kicking over.

Nor does she ever seem to have resented the fact that, from the very beginning, the boundaries of propriety were tightly drawn by the females of the royal house. On one occasion, when she was four, she said, 'My goodness!' in the hearing of her mother, herself a trainee royal, and was at once told that it was *not* a pretty thing to have said and must under no circumstances be repeated. Elizabeth's starchy grandmother, Queen Mary, even took the view that *real* royalty ought not to smile in public, a tenet from which – to judge from the pictures of the period – she herself seldom, if ever, strayed.

Elizabeth grew up in royal splendour. The house in Piccadilly where she spent the first ten years of her life had 25 bedrooms and 18 servants. Both she and her younger sister Margaret, who was born four years later in 1930, had their own nannies. They also had a governess, Marion Crawford ('Crawfie'), who gave them such education as they had in their early years. 'Crawfie' later wrote (in a book *The Little Princesses* which led to her dismissal for breaching family confidentiality) that, while Elizabeth was the sister with the temper, Margaret was always the naughty, if charming, second child.

From the beginning, Elizabeth was protective and indulgent towards her sister. When Margaret did something irritating, she would merely say 'Oh, Margaret!' It was a childish foretaste of their adult relationship. As they and their parents drove back from a wartime visit to the set of Noel Coward's film *In Which We Serve*, Elizabeth – then just fifteen – was profoundly shocked by the way her younger sister mocked the crowds gathered to hear the Royal Family. According to another member of the party, Elizabeth's attitude was: 'If you feel like that, the least you can do is not say it!' I suppose she felt even then 'these are my people!' She was, in fact, already behaving like a head prefect. In later life, she was often to be thoroughly exasperated by Margaret's waywardness and bizarre amours, but the two women remained close until Margaret's death in 2002. Margaret might sometimes be a thorough nuisance, but she was still the Queen's little sister.

Elizabeth probably saw more of her parents than most upper-class children of the period. The Duke and Duchess of York were not part of the international smart set, of which the Duke's brother – the Prince of Wales – was such a prominent member. Unlike him, they were anything but fast. The Duke had a terrible stammer and usually preferred staying at home to going out to parties. Princess Elizabeth's mother taught her to read, told her Bible stories and led family sing-songs round the piano. The Yorks and their children were a very close and genuinely happy foursome.

In adolescence and young womanhood, by which time she was clearly the heir to the throne, Edward VIII having abdicated, Elizabeth's demeanour, both in public and in private, was equally blameless. She never fluffed an engagement but, on social occasions, had something of the wallflower about her. 'If you went with her to a Guards cocktail party,' said Lady Margaret Colville, who became her lady-in-waiting in 1946, 'she was so paralyzed that

she could hardly speak. She really was painfully shy, just lost for words. All the young officers would be round Princess Margaret, who was always the life and soul of the party. There were never many round poor Princess Elizabeth.'

Not that she lacked the normal female sexual emotions. At evening parties in nightspots like the 400 Club in Leicester Square and discreetly squired by young men she found attractive, Elizabeth behaved like any other demure young woman of the period. 'She clearly found Hugh Euston (now the Duke of Grafton), Porchy (Lord Porchester, later Lord Carnarvon) and Lord Plunket sexually attractive,' said another lady-in-waiting, 'and they would get come-hither looks, a fluttering of the eyelashes. You can't have anything much going on between you in a Viennese waltz, but there's the look, the slight pressure of the hand and, in those days, it wasn't so commonplace to want the next thing.'

Anyone who indicated that they might have the next thing in mind was very swiftly rebuffed. 'Charles, the late Duke of Rutland, was one of the young men whom the Queen Mother might have thought of as marrying Elizabeth,' said the late Lord Charteris, who was to be her favourite private secretary when she became Queen, 'and he was certainly very fond of her, but evidently made a pass at her which greatly offended her. I once asked her whether he had done so and there was no answer, which tells its own story!'

To a family friend, who had the neck to ask her the same question, Elizabeth replied tartly, 'There are passes *and* passes!' That made the friend wonder whether it had been an underpass or an overpass. Whichever it was, Elizabeth's relations with Rutland remained rather chilly ever thereafter.

Already, she was the woman she was to remain throughout fifty long and difficult years on the throne – cautious and, above all, in control. Martin Charteris, who served her for twenty-seven years and knew her for fifty, said that the key to her character was that she was actually afraid of her emotions because they were very strong, and always tried to keep them under iron control.

Incredibly, on the royal tour of South Africa in 1947, even those closest to her had no inkling of the fact that she was besotted with Philip Mountbatten, to whom she became engaged later that same year at Balmoral with a rapture so complete that she did not even ask her parents before accepting his proposal. In retrospect, her earlier restraint seems almost inhuman.

Princess Elizabeth, aged two, with the Duchess of York.

'Of course I saw a great deal of her on that trip,' said Lady Colville, 'but I wasn't conscious that she was potty about him. She would never have said, "I haven't had a letter from Philip," or "Oh dear, he's gone off me!" – there was nothing like that to give you a clue. I wouldn't say she was sexy and I wouldn't say she was cool, she was just terribly restrained.'

And she was cautious, always cautious, a woman old, dignified, supremely conscientious beyond her years, no careless abandon, no breathless flights of fancy even at the age of twenty-one. When it came to duty, even in those early days, she was meticulous and swift, unlike her father the King, whose dilatoriness with documents often infuriated politicians, and her mother the Queen, who totally lacked her elder daughter's robotic attention to detail.

Working with her, according to Meg Colville, was like dealing with a businessman. 'For the Princess, routine was bliss. Letters would arrive and be promptly answered – not like Queen Elizabeth, where you'd get no answer and the letters would just disappear.' If there was a problem, the young Elizabeth would spot it and address it. Above all, she would never, ever take a risk. 'She wanted to get everything right,' said Lady Colville, 'and she did.' That, she thought, was not because of the trauma of the Abdication, it was just something deep in Elizabeth's nature.

Yet the departure of Edward VIII, whom his critics understandably regarded as both weak and louche, had been the determining event in the life of Elizabeth's entire family. It had pitched her father into a role for which, temperamentally, he was wholly unsuited and which may have played a part in his early death. It made her mother a widow long before her time and unleashed a bitter family vendetta against the woman who had seduced Edward away. It also rocked the monarchy to its very foundations. That, as Elizabeth saw at first hand, was what happened when people were run by their emotions, lost control of themselves, forgot that duty came first, second and last.

She knew, too, that public confidence in the monarchy had taken time and excruciatingly painful effort to rebuild. Elizabeth's father, after all, had none of the charisma of his elder brother. And there was always the question of how the monarchy could continue to justify its existence in an era when its power was in steep and continuing decline. The answer was that the new King and Queen and their two daughters – 'we four', as Elizabeth's father put it – should be seen as a model family, an exemplar to the nation. They could also avoid making mistakes, behaving badly, causing offence. If Elizabeth had ever had a personal motto, it would have been 'Never put a foot wrong'. The monarchy had just avoided the slippery slope and did not want to venture anywhere near it again.

So self-control, iron, unflagging, superhuman self-control, was to be the order of Elizabeth's reign when she succeeded her father in 1952. Indulgence in emotion of any kind, she believed, could only deflect you from the cool performance of duty. Once you started to express your feelings in public, you revealed your weaknesses, your opinions and, perish the thought, your prejudices, something a constitutional monarch could simply not afford.

In all of this, she was a prize specimen of a British upper class whose character had been shaped to fulfil its imperial role. The thin red line of administrators and soldiers which had somehow held a global empire together would never have survived had the people who ran it allowed their feelings to get the better of them. 'In the centuries when we ruled large parts of the world,' said Sir Antony Jay, who scripted the BBC documentary *Elizabeth R*, 'the upper classes had to develop a shell which fitted them to be Governor-General of India or district commissioner in Tanganyika. It gave them balance, detachment and a very profound coolness. The Queen is one of those people.' Her father, observing these characteristics in her, knew instinctively that she was going to be a stayer, not a sprinter, and shrewdly forecast that she might well be on the throne for as long as her great-grandmother, Queen Victoria.

Elizabeth succeeded in suppressing her emotions to an extent which made even the downiest of Cabinet ministers marvel. 'She has almost,' declared Lord Hurd, the former Tory Foreign Secretary, 'trained feelings out of herself.' Speaking of the Royal Family as a whole, and the Queen in particular, Martin Charteris once drily remarked: 'They do feel things, but they don't feel very much.' Elizabeth's self-control was admirable in its way and, no doubt, she could not have done her job without it, but the cost to her family was to prove terrible. Her eldest son, Prince Charles, in particular, seemed to come a poor second to the formalities which she felt her role demanded. He has never been able to understand the apparent lack of maternal instinct in his mother.

Nevertheless, through the *anni horribiles* of the 1990s, when the Windsors seemed to be challenging for the title of the world's most dysfunctional family, the fact that she had somehow made herself immune to normal human

sensitivities stood her in good stead. It armoured her against the bitter accidents of fortune. The courtiers of the time found her awesomely phlegmatic. 'In my seven years at the Palace as press secretary from 1990 to 1997,' said Charles Anson, 'we had the separation and divorce of both the Waleses and the Yorks, the divorce of Princess Anne and the publication of the book about Diana by Andrew Morton, not to mention the Windsor fire, but the Queen never showed any sign of dejection or depression.

'During those years, I constantly found myself thinking, "What on earth is going to happen today?" You felt as if you were in a tiny sailing boat in a huge storm and that the only thing to do was batten down every hatch, go below and sit it out, but at the centre of the storm was this figure who never lost her serenity. And always, all the time, the same dry, wry sense of humour.

'I remember going with her on a State visit to Paris on the Monday after the first, devastating serialization of the Morton book. Several times during a very busy day I had to ask her advice. "Sorry to trouble you, Ma'am," I'd say, "but this does need an answer." She'd had to shake a thousand people by the hand, but not once was there the slightest hint of annoyance, of "Why are you bothering me at this moment?" And then, having given her answer, the doors would open and the Queen would walk out into the public gaze as if she didn't have a care in the world.'

Those senior courtiers who did see her briefly in the grip of dejection were all the more shocked. 'The only time I saw her looking really shattered,' said one, 'was at Balmoral in 1992, after we'd had the pictures of the Duchess of York having her toes sucked by an American in the South of France plus the publication of some ghastly tapes or other. The Queen was grey and ashen and completely flat. She looked so awful, I felt like crying. I said, "I can't say anything, Ma'am, other than that you will be in my prayers." We were leaving Balmoral the next morning and I was loading up our car when two highly polished Range Rovers appeared with Prince Philip, the Queen, a gamekeeper called Sandy Masson and an equerry. I said to my wife, "We can't not say goodbye," but to our astonishment, when we met her, the Queen was absolutely transformed, smiling and happy. They were going out ferreting as a way of getting rid of the gloom and doom.' Who is to say

Six-year-old Elizabeth with two-year-old Margaret in 1932.

whether the Queen's transformation was an answer to a prayer or the product of her own phlegmatic and resilient temperament?

It is no easy matter to penetrate the Queen's private world and begin to understand what kind of woman she really is. Her defences, both in public and in private, are very heavily fortified. Even Martin Charteris, for all his years by her side, still regarded her as an enigma. Courtiers who worked closely with her for years readily admit that they have no idea of her opinions on a vast range of subjects. They admire her deeply but find her impenetrably delphic.

The difficulty is compounded by the fact that those who have won her confidence sufficiently for her to let her hair down and speak her mind become part of a near-impregnable ring of silence. She has a splendid sense of humour, they claim, but when asked to give examples, they usually remain dumb. To repeat what she has said, even in jest, would – they believe – dishonour both her and the constitution. It is an eighth wonder of the world that none of her ten Prime Ministers has ever leaked what was said in one of the private audiences which they have with her week by week.

Even that most experienced and professional of BBC documentary makers, Edward Mirzoeff, who produced *Elizabeth R*, which marked the fortieth anniversary of the Queen's accession to the throne, confesses that, after a whole year spent with her and her entourage, he still cannot claim to know her. During that year, Mirzoeff twice lunched privately with the Royal Family – once sitting between the Queen and the Queen Mother – talked to the Queen in her private sitting-room, sat with her as she had her portrait painted, went with her to Sandringham and Balmoral; in short, spent far more time with her in intimate situations than all her biographers put together. For almost thirty years before then he had been making documentaries about celebrities of all kinds and, by the time he finished filming them, had always felt that he knew his subject through and through. Not so on this occasion. Of course, he said, he had come to know the Queen's mannerisms and the style of her daily behaviour, but the woman herself remained a mystery.

That was partly because, unlike so many of his other celebrities, the seductive power of the camera did not turn the Queen's head in any way. 'She isn't at all vain,' he said. 'She was perfectly ready to appear in circumstances which no vain person would have tolerated.' He was not to know it, but not once either during or after the filming did the Queen ask members of her staff, 'How did I do?' That, perhaps, was why the entire BBC crew felt that they were her subjects and not she theirs. Even in such seductive circumstances, monarchy can still retain its magic.

Mirzoeff's crew were all expected to bow each time they met the Queen.There was nothing strange in that. From the beginning of her life she had always been surrounded by formality. When Lady Elizabeth Cavendish, the Duke of Devonshire's sister and one of the late Princess Margaret's ladies-in-waiting, went to Buckingham Palace at the age of eleven to play games and have tea with Princess Elizabeth, she had to curtsey and call her 'Ma'am'. 'It was,' she recalls, 'a very inhibiting experience. Although we played a lot together when we were children, and she has always called me Elizabeth, I have never called her Lilibet.'

The stories told by those close to the Queen reveal the sometimes raw reality of the relationship between Elizabeth and her husband. 'Prince Philip and the Queen have truly phenomenal rows while we're around,' one retired courtier told me, 'and it really is very embarrassing. When you first hear it, you can hardly believe it. "This is ridiculous . . . Why on earth are you doing that? . . . Where have you been, you've no idea what you're talking about . . . Come on, Lilibet, you're talking rubbish!" There's a terrific mutual tongue-lashing and then they'll end up the best of friends.' The Queen is perfectly capable of giving as good as she gets. Once, she and Prince Philip were being briefed in the Cabinet Office about the situation of British troops in Bosnia. Philip, who reckons to be the family expert on military matters, asked whether Britain would be able to pull out all its equipment should it decide to withdraw. 'You must be joking!' snapped the Queen briskly.

For all her self-control, the royal temper – though it shows itself but rarely – is still in good working order. 'I only once saw her really lose her temper,' said Lord Charteris, 'and that was when Mobutu, one of those African politicians [he was, in fact, the Zairian President] came to Britain on a State visit with his wife in 1973.

'They were accommodated in Buckingham Palace. We soon discovered that Mrs Mobutu had brought with her a filthy little dog which she had smuggled through Customs in a muff. She actually ordered it some steak! They'd turned their whole suite into a caravanserai. When the Queen heard about it, she said with tremendous force, "Martin, that dog is to be out of my house by three

o'clock this afternoon!" She was really shaking with anger. Someone from Customs came to pick the creature up.'

Some of the stories told by those close to the Queen reveal another, infinitely less inhibited, woman who lurks behind the cool and often daunting public façade. Occasionally that other woman emerges, to the amazement even of those who have known her for decades. The visit of Gough Whitlam, the Australian Labour Prime Minister, to Windsor with his wife Margaret on Good Friday, 1973, was one such occasion. Even as he told the astonishing story of what happened after dinner that night, Lord Charteris wondered if he had been dreaming and simply imagined it. He had not. Gough Whitlam remembers the evening only too well. So does another senior courtier who was also there.

'When Whitlam came to power in 1972,' recalled Charteris, 'the Queen didn't know him and there was talk that Australians would no longer be singing "God Save the Queen" or taking an oath of loyalty to the sovereign. We even wondered if Whitlam wanted to move Australia towards a republic. The Queen and I talked about it and we decided that I should see the Australian High Commissioner with the message that Whitlam could of course do whatever he chose but that, if anything he had in mind affected the Queen, she expected to be informed. Three days later, the High Commissioner telephoned to say that Whitlam would like to see the Queen and, in due course, he arrived at Windsor with his wife – Big Marge, as we affectionately called her.

'He had brought with him as a present a huge sheepskin rug in an absolutely enormous soft leather suitcase,' recalled the other senior courtier who was there. 'There was a lot of unconfined mirth after dinner that night and I think we must have had a fair amount to drink. When the sheepskin rug had been spread on the floor of the Great Drawing-Room, the Queen said that the suitcase was so big, she could get into it. She was in a very playful, teasing mood and Gough, as I recall, made an effort to wrap the rug around her.'

Princess Margaret evidently also got down onto the rug with the Queen. In a magazine diary, Mrs Gough Whitlam later wrote, 'You would have loved the sight of the sisters sitting side by side on the deep-piled, cream sheepskin rug we gave Her Majesty. They looked like "the Little Princesses" on either one's teenage birthday.'

King George VI and Queen Elizabeth with the two princesses at the Welsh House, Windsor Castle, 1936.

'Neither the Queen nor I knew whether Whitlam intended to declare a republic,' Charteris went on, 'but that evening she was quite determined to catch her man. A lot of her sexuality has been suppressed but, that night, she used it like a weapon. She wrapped Gough Whitlam round her little finger, knocked him sideways. She sat on that rug in front of him, stroked it and said how lovely it was. It was an arrant use of sexuality. I was absolutely flabbergasted. Afterwards, Whitlam said, "Well, if she's like that, it's all right by me!" '

Whether the Queen's performance knocked Whitlam sideways or not, he told me that it reminded him of Antony's first sight of Cleopatra. He also recalls noticing that the Queen has a good pair of legs. For the time being, at least, there was no further talk of a republic.

So the Queen is a woman of flesh and blood just as we are. But how good a Queen has she been thus far, over the long years since she ascended the throne in 1952? What has she contributed to the new Elizabethan Age we were promised then? And how good a mother has she been? – a no less important question, since the head of a royal house, like the head of any great landed family, has one prime duty: to pass on what they have received to the next generation in better shape than it was when they received it. In the Queen's case, is the standing of the monarchy higher than it was in 1952? And if not, why not?

Half a century ago, long before it became a matter of general concern, she faced, in its most extreme form, the dilemma of every career woman: how to juggle job and family so that neither is neglected. The Queen never aspired to be a superwoman, but she certainly had it all – vast wealth, a quiverful of magnificent homes, platoons of servants, an attractive husband and children, an inheritance undefiled save for the temporary aberration of the Abdication, not to mention a satisfying though relentlessly demanding job. It was a truly Herculean challenge. How has she measured up to it?

In the early years, everything seemed to be in her favour: youth, beauty, a dream family and the deferential adoration of subjects around the globe. But, as the years went by, the sky grew ever darker. Her family spewed forth a series of squalid affairs and divorces. A tidal wave of tacky revelations soiled the monarchy's image. A pack of sensation-hungry journalists hunted down their every gaffe, and there were gaffes a-plenty. The Windsors became the media's favourite soap opera, in the minds of the Queen's own subjects an upper-class version of *Peyton Place*, as Martin Charteris once remarked.

The Royal Family, most obligingly, even wrote their own script, not to mention publishing their own self-revelatory books and TV confessions. In a high-tech age, where little was sacred and even less private, they began to be seen as just another bunch of celebrities, although their uniquely elevated status ought to have set them completely apart.

The hierarchy of splendour was turned on its head. Beside the glitter, albeit transient, of a host of pinchbeck luminaries – footballers, talk-show hosts, pop stars – the Queen, as she grew older, began to seem dull, dowdy and anachronistic. Only Princess Diana and her sons matched up to the demand for youth, glamour and pazazz. This reversal of status was a matter of the deepest concern to even the most loyal of the Queen's servants. Before he died, Martin Charteris was profoundly worried about the monarchy's future and, in his heart of hearts, wondered just what sort of future it had.

Criticism of the Queen's performance, both as monarch and mother, comes from both expected and unexpected quarters. Lady Elizabeth Longford, one of the Queen's most admiring biographers, says that while she may not have put a foot wrong, she could also be charged with not having put a foot forward. Loyal courtiers freely admit that, while the Queen may have what they call 'splendid negative judgement' (i.e. knowing what *not* to do), she is also totally lacking in imagination.

Infinitely more damaging, one of Princes Charles's closest aides maintains that 'in some ways, the Queen has behaved as if she is the only one who matters. She almost seems to see herself as the last sovereign. She has certainly not planned for the future terribly well. Everything has been what is good for her, not what is good for the monarchy in the long term. Prince Charles feels frustrated at not being allowed to be involved enough because although he is the heir to the throne, his mother treats him no differently from his siblings.' In fact, according to his own aides, Charles often feels like little more than a fringe player while the monarchy – with his father's hand still firmly on the tiller – goes to pot.

Family rivalries apart, there are fierce critics from the heart of the Establishment who, while acknowledging the Queen's virtues, believe that in crucial respects she has fallen woefully short. 'She's been a wonderful Queen in the sense of duty, discipline, dignity and the grace with which she has conducted her duties,' said a very senior civil servant. 'Although she looks forbidding,

kindness is there and so is the skill which enables her to keep out of trouble. And she has an amazing touch for being able to convey disapproval when she has been put in an undignified position. The look of utter distaste on her face when she was required to sing "Auld Lang Syne" at the Millennium Dome on New Year's Day 2000 spoke volumes.

'However, because she has been so punctilious about keeping out of politics, she has reduced the monarchy to a position where it hardly matters and where most people wouldn't notice if it disappeared. She should have exerted herself more. I am not uncritical of the Prince of Wales, but he has taken chances and often spoken for the people. She has never done that. He has made a real difference, whereas it's difficult to think of things where *she* has. She's just played it absolutely safe. It's rather like the parable of the talents, safely buried below the ground but not flourishing sufficiently above it. She should have taken more risks. So I'm afraid she comes across as a rather dull monarch, although she is not at all dull to be with.'

David Starkey, the well-known historian, is equally scathing. 'When she arrived,' he said, 'we were promised a new Elizabethan Age but, although she's been quite extraordinarily dutiful, the Queen – unlike the first Elizabeth – is utterly uneducated. She has also been very badly served by her advisers. She seems to have regarded it as her duty to keep the monarchy as it was. At the time of the Abdication, the Royal Family decided they didn't like modernity – and, with all his faults, Edward VIII was modern in dress and behaviour – and came down in favour of the George V/Queen Mary model. So times changed, but the Queen didn't. It's as if the Conservative Party was stuck in the age of Stanley Baldwin. Until the Silver Jubilee in 1977 she was extremely successful, but, since then, the monarchy has had twenty-five of the worst years of its history, and I think the Queen is significantly to blame.'

The case for the defence is put equally strongly by the Queen's many fervent admirers. 'You simply *cannot* lay the failure of the new Elizabethan Age at the feet of the Queen,' retorted a civil servant who was private secretary to three Prime Ministers. 'A constitutional sovereign cannot be a success if her government is a failure and, although things like the Welfare State and the National Health Service were jewels in the national crown when she came to the throne, those jewels were

Elizabeth gets down to it, changing a wheel while in the ATS, April 1945.

very soon either recognized as paste or became tarnished. Their underpinning was an economy in decline. Our politicians and their officials always thought we could do more than we could, and were always living in the past in so many ways. You cannot blame the Queen for those failures. And one of the good things about *this* Elizabethan Age has been the transition from Empire to Commonwealth. In that, the Queen has played a very significant part.'

That transition has been far from seamless but, unlike several other imperial powers, Britain has somehow retained its position as the focus of an extremely assorted family of nations. Some of the Queen's British Prime Ministers have had little patience with the Commonwealth, and its value has often been questioned, but – despite the fact that some of its members have acted deplorably – it has set a standard of behaviour which the vast majority abide by. It is also an invaluable bridge between the developed and developing worlds. Nations such as Mozambique which were never part of the British Empire think enough of this curious family to join it. Nelson Mandela brought South Africa back into the Commonwealth as soon as he became President. Yet, without Elizabeth's enthusiasm and winning ways, it might not have survived for so long.

What is more, argue her defenders, the Queen has been a model of good behaviour and flawless duty, a rock of sanity in difficult times. In the view of Lord Donoughue, the former Labour minister, she is simply the finest monarch we have ever had. 'She is pure gold,' declared one of her former private secretaries, 'and, as someone told me when I first arrived at the Palace, a wonderful colleague. She has bailed me out of a lot of bad judgements, I can tell you.'

Her presence, her supporters add, is very widely felt in public life. She may have almost no constitutional power, though she does have the right to be consulted, to advise and to warn; and has certainly never meddled in politics, as virtually all her predecessors did. She is, apparently, as free from political bias as she plainly is from racial prejudice. On the other hand, largely because of her restrained behaviour and her blameless personal life, she has exercised a curious and rather pervasive influence over both the Establishment and the would-be Establishment who covet both her good opinion and the honours which can flow from it.

'She has never set the country on fire,' said the late Lord Charteris, 'but she is a wonderful person to serve, a very faithful, honourable, arrow-straight person who will never let you down. And she won't ever put on an act. She once told me: "If people don't like me as I am, they had better find somebody else, because it is not honourable to be otherwise." When I drafted a speech which required her to say, "I'm very glad to be in Birmingham today," she crossed out the *very*. She is very strong, she is not going to be blown off course for anybody or anything, and she has a deep and enduring sense of her duty and destiny.'

'He's just the man for the job'

2 Elizabeth and Philip

As a young woman, Elizabeth did not need much, but she did need a husband. Heirs to thrones are, at the very least, expected to produce heirs of their own, and the sooner the better. Her mother, the Queen, was thoroughly seized of the fact, and made a point of marshalling as much of the available talent as she could.

'Queen Elizabeth,' said Sir Edward Ford, assistant private secretary to King George, 'wanted to introduce her daughter to a wide range of possibles from the higher flights of the British aristocracy. Her own favourite might have been Hugh Euston, but there were other people like Johnny Dalkeith, heir to the Duke of Buccleuch, and Sonny Blandford, the Duke of Marlborough's heir, both of whom had acres aplenty (270,000 in Dalkeith's case). Simon Phipps, later the Bishop of Lincoln, came to stay quite a bit. So did Lord Brabourne (who later married Lady Mountbatten). The Queen wanted Elizabeth to see a lot of young men, any of whom might have been suitable if they fell for each other. You'd often find three or four of them staying at Sandringham or Balmoral at the same time.'

As the newspapers began to realize that a little preliminary matchmaking was under way, the gossip factories began to hum. Elizabeth's name was linked with all kinds of young men, some of whom were quite surprised – and perhaps even a little alarmed – to be regarded as candidates for her hand. Had he ever thought of marrying her, I once asked the Duke of Grafton? Grafton was one of five Grenadier Guards officers who had stayed at Windsor with the Royal Family during the war and regularly had lunch with the two young princesses. 'Good Lord, no!' he replied. 'When one of the London evening papers rang to ask if it was true that we were engaged, my father said, "Go to hell!" and slammed the phone down.' Grafton had perhaps seen enough of court life not to want to be mewed up in it for the rest of his days.

And then, as Elizabeth's mother was only too well aware, there was Philip Mountbatten. Elizabeth had first met him just before the war, at the age of thirteen, and it soon became clear that he meant much more to her than any of her 'flirts', as she called them. He was strikingly good-looking, the pin-up boy of bevies of adoring public schoolgirls. 'We used to sing a little jingle,' recalled one of the Queen Mother's family, blushing at the memory. ' "Oh come to my arms, thou bundle of charms, Philip Mountbatten R.N." We were all in love with him.' Elizabeth, though, could see a great deal more in him than looks.

To begin with, Philip was very much his own man, in awe of no one, strikingly independent and saltily outspoken. He totally lacked the courtly, understated manners of the English country gentleman. Nor did he seem bound by the conventions which Elizabeth herself slavishly observed. And he was certainly no eager, fawning suitor. As one former courtier put it, 'He was not all over her, and she found that very attractive.' On the contrary, there was something of the wild stallion about him. His raw energy and uninhibited behaviour spoke to a side of Elizabeth which had seldom been allowed to express itself. This shy, reserved young woman desperately needed bringing out of herself and Philip was just the man for the job.

What is more, in terms of sheer blood, he was at least on her level, literally in a class by himself. He was not only a great-great-great-grandson of Queen Victoria and second cousin to her own father but also, for what it was worth, related to the royal families of Russia, Prussia, Denmark and Greece: even, it was claimed, a descendant of Charlemagne. 'Not to put too fine a point of it,' said his cousin, Lady Mountbatten, 'he is far more royal than the Queen.'

Given that sort of lineage, he was unlikely to let himself be pushed around by Buckingham Palace's pompous and formidable Old Guard. Many of the other candidates were decent enough, but they were scarcely men of destiny. Elizabeth could admire Philip, look up to him. He made her go weak at the knees. She could choose no other and, as it turned out, would allow no other to be chosen for her. So far as she was concerned, he was the biological imperative made flesh.

None of this pleased Elizabeth's mother one little bit. She did not much care for Philip. That, perhaps, was why she rustled up as many alternative candidates as possible. 'Queen Elizabeth found Philip cold and lacking in our kind of sense of humour,' said one of Princess Elizabeth's ladies-in-waiting. 'He wasn't able to see the ridiculous side of things, and that is perhaps rather Germanic. And he certainly didn't set out to charm her.' She sensed that he might turn out to be an awkward and disruptive customer, certainly not as biddable as a home-grown country gentleman. That, moreover, was a good deal less than half of it. Queen Elizabeth was also very suspicious of the fact that Philip's uncle, Lord Louis Mountbatten, was his main sponsor. She thought, quite rightly, that Mountbatten was a man on the make. After all, might not Philip be the Trojan horse who would try to transform the House of Windsor into the House of Mountbatten? 'The Queen had produced a cricket eleven of possibles,' said Edward Ford, 'and it's hard to know whom she would have sent in first, but it certainly wouldn't have been Philip!'

Just who was this extraordinary man? His childhood could scarcely have been more different than Elizabeth's. A woman who was later to become one of the Queen Mother's ladies-in-waiting shrewdly remarked that 'given the way he was brought up, it really is a miracle that he is normal'. Philip's childhood certainly helps to explain his later behaviour and, in particular, the way in which he dealt with his own children.

By the time he was eight years old, his parents had been exiled from Greece, where they had been part of a royal family imported from Denmark as recently as 1863, so Philip had neither homeland nor home. He had also effectively been deserted by his mother, Princess Alice, who spent eight years in German and Swiss sanatoria suffering from what doctors diagnosed as 'paranoid schizophrenia' and by his philandering father, Prince Andrew, who went off to live with a mistress in Monte Carlo. From the age of eight until he was fifteen, Philip never saw his mother or even had a birthday card from her. Today, even with close friends, he still finds it difficult to talk about her.

At school in England, first at Cheam and then at Gordonstoun, Philip was seldom visited by relatives. In the holidays, he was parcelled out around the palaces

and country houses of the family. His four sisters had all married German princelings, and so his summers were often spent at their colossal piles. In England, there were the homes of the Mountbattens and their relatives by marriage, the Wernhers.

'Looking back at my childhood,' Philip once said to a woman friend, 'it really is amazing that I was left to cross a continent all by myself – taxis, trains, boats – to get to my sisters' homes in Germany. There was nobody to take me, nobody to pick me up.' To the friend, he sounded just like a little orphan. As a child, Princess Elizabeth had been indulged in all kinds of ways. Philip had certainly not.

'I first met him when he was eight,' said Lady Georgina Kennard, Sir Harold Wernher's elder daughter. 'He spent a lot of time at our country house at Thorpe Lubbenham in Leicestershire. He was very rumbustious, full of fun, kicking everything he saw. He once kicked me down a few stairs. But he did have a terribly sad background. He had no home to go to, nobody to kiss him goodnight, nobody to help him pack his trunk, nobody to take him back to school, nobody much to go and see him when he was at school. He never whinged, but it must have been awful not to have love.

'In those days, he only had the coat he stood up in and certainly no suit, because my parents bought him one. Father, who was a very successful businessman, also paid a good part of his school fees, though other people chipped in as well. With Philip, it was never ever "Poor me!" but he did once say, "Where is home? Except for all of you, I don't have a home to come back to."'

'The effect of not having a home is imponderable,' said Lady Kennard's younger sister Myra, now Lady Butter. 'You didn't go into that sort of thing in those days but now people like Philip would be counselled all the time. I'm sure, though that, because the Mountbattens and ourselves had to look after him financially, he felt beholden. That made him all the more determined to be a success and, above all else, to keep his independence.'

Those who know Philip well believe that, in his youth, he developed a well-nigh impenetrable defence mechanism to hide the hurt that the absence of parents inevitably caused him. 'My feeling about him,' said his cousin Lady Mountbatten, 'is that he has a much more sensitive centre than people have ever understood, because he's had to build a hard shell around himself to survive the circumstances in which his life has been lived.'

Elizabeth and Philip leaving Westminster Abbey after the wedding ceremony, 20 November 1947.

'His childhood experience taught him to be cautious, to swallow his gentler feelings,' remarked his friend Michael Mann, the former Dean of Windsor, 'and what he did was build a picket line around himself with machine-guns on it. You are not admitted through that line unless you are totally trusted.'

'Once you've been hurt by not having a home,' said a veteran courtier who saw very little of his own parents during his childhood, 'you're going to make damn sure you're not hurt again. You learn to be wary of telling people how you feel, because there is no one to tell who you're sure will understand. That's why Prince Philip does not find it easy to communicate at an emotional level. He also, like the Queen, hates physical contact.'

Later, Philip's oldest friends and aides were to be puzzled about the root cause of his often unpredictable behaviour and hair-trigger reactions. 'You never knew when it was going to come,' said the late Commander Michael Parker, who became his equerry, 'and I wondered if he hadn't been with his mother enough, or was it the insecurity of never having had a home? He never said a word about his family in all the years I was with him. He was very bottled up on that subject. I'd sense these things but, when I'd say, "Are you terribly upset at not having a home?" he'd say, "What the bloody hell are you talking about?" I still don't know if I was hitting the mark, but he is very self-contained person who hates revealing any kind of vulnerability.' Parker clearly felt like a dentist who had hit a raw nerve.

Jimmy Taylor, the son of Philip's headmaster at Cheam (to which he went in 1930), saw the beginnings of this extraordinarily self-contained character. 'Even then,' he told me, 'Philip was a very private person. He neither gave confidences away nor welcomed them. He had to be very self-contained because he couldn't rely on anyone to visit him like the other boys. My father Harold became his guardian since he had no other male close enough to hold his hand when he needed one. Curiously enough, none of these emotional factors, the things that affect the psyche, surface in the biographies which have been written about him, but he'd be a fascinating person for a psychologist to get to work on.'

'He was known at Cheam as Flop,' recalled John Wynne, a school friend, 'and he had absolutely no side, he was not at all pompous, unlike his cousin the Earl of Medina who was there at the same time. He was very good at sports of all kinds – he was the first eleven goalkeeper – and when you think of all the problems he had being shovelled around, it was a remarkable achievement. He wasn't bullied. Nobody would ever have taken a poke at him, because they'd have got one back!

'When we were both eleven and a half or twelve, we dead-heated in the high jump and, at the prizegiving, I pushed him forward to go and collect the cup. When he came back, he gave it to me. "That's yours," he said. He had tremendous confidence from somewhere.' Even then, with no money and few possessions, Philip had no interest in collecting trophies and acquiring material things.

Wynne was given a clue to Philip's apparent confidence just before they both left Cheam. 'We were unpacking our trunks in the dorm,' he recalled, 'and I saw that in his, right at the bottom under a pair of underpants or a towel, he had a photograph of King George the Fifth which said, "From Uncle George". He had never displayed it.'

'He's descended from everybody he should be descended from,' said one of Prince Charles's former private secretaries, 'but there is a great big hole where there should be Mummy picking him up after a party and giving him a kiss. Prince Philip did not have the chance to learn the tricks of the trade of domestic bliss.'

Whatever the other effects of his childhood experience, Philip has certainly paid a price in emotional terms for his inability to cope with warmth and intimacy – and being able to transmit them. He is only too aware of that lack in himself. Talking to a friend, he once said: 'I don't seem able to say nice things to people, though I would like to. Why is that?'

He also, apparently, has a sense of insecurity about his own identity. He was once talking to a courtier about adopted children and the fact that they often do not know who they are. The courtier, who comes from a very close family, confessed that he could not imagine anyone not knowing who they were. 'But look at me,' retorted Philip. 'I used to wonder who I was.' Then the veil came down again.

As a young man, he sometimes referred to himself as Philip of Greece, and yet Greece had rejected his family. He none the less clung to a link which was utterly tenuous: he had no Greek blood in his veins at all. Harold Taylor, his headmaster at Cheam, used to get Christmas cards from him signed Phillipos, with the Greek version underneath, but both he and his son Jimmy wondered just how Greek Philip really was. By the time he reached Cheam, he spoke French fluently as a second language after English, and often won the French prize. He picked up German later on visits to his sisters and during a year he spent at school in Germany. His Greek has always been extremely rudimentary.

The Greek connection did not even provide him with a surname. 'The Greek Royal Family is unique in not having one,' said a close friend, 'so he was really

the Prince of Nothing, the Prince of Nowhere.' Eventually, he was to take the name of the English branch of his family, Mountbatten (itself an anglicized version of Battenberg), but none of the people I have talked to think of him as being in any way English. As he himself points out to friends, he is a first-generation immigrant to this country. 'Identity and roots he never had,' said Lady Butter.

'Prince Philip,' observed Rabbi Arthur Herzberg, a distinguished American writer who has talked at length to him, 'is the Gentile version of the assimilated Jew. He was abandoned and decided that he had to make it on his own, but does not know who he is. He has lost his real identity. He once told me that he thinks of himself as a cosmopolitan European.'

At Gordonstoun, where he eventually became head boy (Guardian), Philip showed himself to be a natural leader with a sense of fun. 'He didn't have to shout or be severe,' recalled Lord Gainford, who was a pupil at the same time, 'he just had a way of getting boys to do what needed to be done without having to roar. He kept good order by his personality. He was also big and tough, so nobody was going to take him on physically. He didn't seem to worry about the fact that he never had any visitors. He was very well liked because he was full of go, one of the lads. I never knew he was a prince. There was a delicious amount of the devil in him.'

These, then, were the beginnings of the man who, in 1947, was to marry the future Queen. She, still a teenager, had spent most of the war at Windsor Castle, while Philip had had a distinguished war in the Royal Navy. He had fought in the battle of Matapan. He had been mentioned in despatches for bravery. He was not, however, regarded as any sort of hero by many of those who witnessed his arrival at Balmoral in the summer of 1946 when it was becoming clear that the Prince of Nowhere was about to become the Prince of somewhere very close at hand.

It turned out to be a fascinating stand-off between the British Establishment's old guard and an impecunious naval officer who, astonishingly, made no attempt to ingratiate himself with any of them.

'I first met Philip in the summer of that year,' said Sir Edward Ford, 'when everybody was starting to say, "This is going to be it." He behaved with the self-confidence of a naval officer who'd had a good war. He never showed the respect that an English boy of his age would have had for the older people around. He had no retiring graces and wasn't in the least afraid to tell the King's friend Lord Salisbury what he felt.

Elizabeth and Philip at Broadlands on their honeymoon.

Everybody thought, "This rough diamond, will he treat the Princess with the sensitivity she deserves?"'

A good many of those at Balmoral that summer, according to one of the Queen Mother's nieces, Mrs Margaret Rhodes, regarded Philip as 'a foreign interloper out for the goodies', but that was not Ford's impression. 'He hadn't got anything,' he went on, 'not even much in the way of clothes. I think the King sent him to his tailor and more or less kitted him out. But he was not greedy or grasping in any way, out for the baubles, unlike some of the people who've married into the Royal Family since.

'Nor was he going to plead the pauper. He didn't have much in his bank balance, but he never said, "I haven't got a bean," just to excite sympathy. He was perfectly genuine and wasn't out to impress either the younger or the older people.' Mrs Rhodes came to exactly the same judgement. 'He's not interested in money,' she said, 'and certainly wouldn't have bothered to suck up to anybody. I once talked to him about money and he said he didn't need anything except to buy clothes.'

That was an embarrassment which he only revealed to naval chums. 'I remember Philip saying that he was rather ashamed at the look on the face of the footman who was laying out his clothes at Balmoral and Sandringham,' recalled Admiral William O'Brien, who was with him just before the engagement while Philip was an instructor at the Petty Officers' School in Corsham. 'At that point he depended a lot on his grandmother, the Dowager Marchioness of Milford Haven, who I think paid his bills at Gieves, where all naval officers went for their uniforms.'

Philip was at Sandringham for Christmas of that year and, according to John Gibson, who was a footman there at the time, even had to borrow a bow-tie before coming down to dinner. He wore heavily repaired clothes handed down from his father, who had died in the south of France in 1944.

Philip, however, was far from overawed by the royal palaces. 'He was not at all impressed by either Balmoral or Buckingham Palace,' said Mike Parker. 'The shooting lodges of some of the German castles where he spent summer holidays as a boy with his sisters' families are bigger than the royal residences in Britain. You could fit Buckingham Palace into the Margrave of Baden's place at Salem three times over.'

To courtiers such as Peter (now Sir Peter) Ashmore, then the King's equerry, the hostility of many of those present towards Philip was only too obvious. 'The old guard found him hard to swallow. The Eldons and the Salisburys, who were close friends of the King and Queen, ganged up against him and made it plain that they hoped they were not going to let their daughter marry this chap. None of the aristocrats and Old Etonians round the table were in favour of him.'

Despite Philip's war record, some of them wrote him off as thoroughly Teutonic, partly because of all his German in-laws, partly because of his sometimes brusque behaviour. In some cases, the anguish of the First World War still coloured their judgement. After all, Fergus Bowes-Lyon, the Queen's brother, had been killed at Loos. 'David Bowes-Lyon, another of her brothers, to whom she was very much in hock,' said a courtier who was there, 'would simply have said, "He's a German," and the same went for his other detractors.' Queen Elizabeth privately sympathized with her brother's view but was careful not to show her disapproval too openly.

Nor did Philip make any attempt to recruit sympathizers. 'He must have felt the general anti atmosphere,' said Ashmore, 'but he didn't encourage one to be a confidant. He never said, "I can't get on with the bloody lot!" even if he'd thought it. If one had offered help, he might have found it rather patronizing. He was very self-reliant. His childhood had probably made him so. He minded his Ps and Qs with the King and Queen but, even there, he was not the future son-in-law making up to his prospective in-laws.'

To those who were at Balmoral in 1946, there did not seem anything remotely lovey-dovey about the couple who were the subject of so much speculation. Not that that was unusual in an era when it was thought unseemly for people to canoodle in public. 'They certainly did not drool over each other at Balmoral,' recalls Ashmore. 'They scarcely held hands.' Philip, it turned out, was just as undemonstrative in public as the Princess.

'He's not a person who shows love,' said one of the ladies present. 'Elizabeth was probably fonder of him than he was of her but, in any case, he doesn't betray much affection, does he? He's very self-contained. Maybe his feelings were stunted as a child. Given the sort of experience he'd had, you probably would shut yourself away a bit to avoid being hurt again. Affection is not his natural currency.'

In any case, Philip – as a relative put it – had already, unlike Elizabeth, 'played the field'. He had been fond of several women, including a Canadian called Osla Benning, and in love with at least two. The first was Georgina Wernher, now Lady Kennard, with whom he had often been out dining and dancing at places like Quaglino's and the 400 Club.

'My mother always said that Philip's mother would have been very happy for me to have married him,' recalled Lady Kennard, 'but we were both too young and he never asked me. It was a tremendous friendship, he was my best friend in the world. I thought he was marvellously clever and amusing, and I loved being with him. Good-looking? He was astronomical, but I was terribly naive and disciplined, and we all behaved in those days. Girls certainly did.'

The other woman with whom Philip was deeply smitten was Deborah, one of the famous Mitford girls, who is now Duchess of Devonshire. He danced with her a good deal before she married the Duke. The correctness of Philip's behaviour towards her may be measured by the fact that she was astonished (and indeed rather pleased) to be told, quite recently, that he had been in love with her.

All that, however, was in the past. Philip was about to become engaged to an adoring young Princess who was stunningly beautiful and could deploy a smile that was to overwhelm many a happily married courtier. Even if not as besotted as she was, he clearly loved Elizabeth. Marriage to her also offered him things he had longed for all his life. 'I think he'd always thought how marvellous it would be to have a home and family,' said Gina Kennard, 'and he knew there would be a home of real security with Elizabeth.' Mike Parker had the same impression. 'The thing he was most looking for when he came to Britain was a home, a sense that "my anchor can go in right here". So, when he told me in 1946 that he'd become engaged to Elizabeth, he was extremely content, though not way over the top.'

As for the Princess, 'She was mad about him,' one of their closest friends told me, 'though she never showed her feelings in public. She needed someone like him, someone who was his own man, and she realized it.' The royal world, in any case, was where Philip felt most at home, the world for which he was fitted by both birth and character. He may also have thought that marriage to Elizabeth would help restore his own family's reputation after all their sadness and ill-fortune.

On the other hand, he knew only too well that becoming part of this particular Royal Family was unlikely to be a bed of roses. King George had taken a liking to him, they had shot together, and he had said: 'Always come to me if there is anything bothering you with the family.' Neither of the principal royal women, however, showed the least fondness for him. Princess Margaret felt, and said to friends, that he was simply not good enough for her sister. The Court was another black cloud on the horizon, determined to put him in what it fancied to be his place. And Philip knew that, sooner or later, his days as a free spirit would be over and he would have to give himself to a life of relentless royal duty.

These fears loomed ever larger as the wedding day approached in 1947. His nervousness was obvious to his friends in the Thursday Club, an informal all-male affair which met over lunch in Old Compton Street for uninhibited high jinks and bawdy stories. 'At the party which the photographer Baron gave there for Philip before he married,' the late Larry Adler told me, 'he was obviously scared. His face was absolutely white. He said to me, "I suppose I won't be having fun any more."'

After breakfast on the day of the wedding, he found himself alone with his cousin Lady Mountbatten at Kensington Palace, where his grandmother had an apartment. Lady Mountbatten (Lord Louis' elder daughter) said what a great day it was for him. Philip replied apprehensively: 'I don't know if I'm being very brave or very foolish.'

'He was marrying the girl he loved,' she explained, 'but knew that he was going into the lion's den. He was very conscious of the way he'd been treated and how hard he would have to fight for his position and his independence. What he didn't know was just how fearsome it was going to be.' Philip gave up smoking from the day of the wedding to please Elizabeth, who is a non-smoker. It was not to be the only thing he gave up.

On the morning of the wedding, there were only the traditional last-minute hitches to negotiate. After a frantic search, the spray of orchids which Elizabeth was to wear were found in a refrigerator – thoughtfully put there by a nursery footman. A jeweller had to be found to repair the frame of Queen Elizabeth's sunray tiara; and the Princess's double string of pearls, which had been left behind, were hastily fetched from St James's.

With the benefit of hindsight, both the courtiers of the day and their successors can see how shrewd Elizabeth's choice was, and for all kinds of reasons. 'Philip was much better than someone with difficult commitments,' said Edward Ford. 'He came with no baggage in any sense. If the Queen had married Hugh Euston or Johnny Dalkeith, they'd have brought their families with them, some of whom might have been offended if they weren't invited to events. Philip's German relations, by contrast, were only ever going to make the occasional visit.'

'Let's suppose she'd married Dalkeith, who then inherited those colossal estates,' said another former courtier. 'Could he always have been there for her? He might have found himself saying, "I know I ought to be in Leeds with

Lilibet, but this is an absolutely crucial day on the estate at Drumlanrig." Philip had no such encumbrances. He wasn't going to be looking over his shoulder all the time at his other responsibilities. His only encumbrance was his character. Then again, because he himself had royal blood in his veins, he wasn't going to be dazzled by her high status, still less deferential. Dalkeith and Euston wouldn't have given her the sort of ginger she's always got from him.

'What's more, if she'd married Hugh Euston, her other boyfriends like Porchy (the late Lord Carnarvon) would have been as sick as mud, and that might have set up rivalries for the Court of the future. Philip had no one to rival him. He had nothing to lose but himself, and he didn't know what that was anyway!'

One of the Queen Mother's First XI of suitors now has no doubt that Elizabeth married the right man. 'Philip may not be an English gentleman,' the Duke of Grafton told me, 'but I can't think of anyone else who could have done that job.' Richard Chartres, the Bishop of London, put the point with characteristic bluntness and accuracy. 'If one of the standard English aristocrats had married the Queen,' he declared, 'it would have bored everybody out of their minds!' Whatever Philip might be, he was never going to be boring.

The first years of marriage were among the happiest of their lives. 'Philip had a capacity for love which was waiting to be unlocked,' said Lady Mountbatten, 'and Elizabeth unlocked it. In the early days, they were very cosy, very giggly. Once, when just a few of us were sitting together, I said that I'd only just realized what a marvellous complexion she had. Philip laughed and said, "Yes, and she's like that all over!"

'The bore for a young couple who were so much in love was that they'd constantly find the valet or the lady's maid intruding. When Elizabeth was changing for dinner and having a bath, dear old Bobo MacDonald, her dresser, would be in and out of the bathroom, so Philip couldn't share the bath with her. Elizabeth didn't feel she could say, "Bobo, please don't come in," so Philip had to go off and have a bath on his own.'

'He must have had a hell of a time with Bobo,' agreed Mike Parker. 'She was a tyrannical old lady, Princess Elizabeth was her baby and nobody else was going to get anywhere. She was *always* there! So he goes into that Buckingham Palace atmosphere with Bobo in command. It was an awful situation. But do you think he ever said a word? Not once did he groan or complain in my hearing.'

With Clarence House still not ready for them to move into, Elizabeth had her first baby, Prince Charles, at Buckingham Palace in November 1948. Philip was playing squash while she was having her contractions, but was brought from the Palace court immediately after the delivery. By that time, the crowd outside the Palace had become so large that the police had to cordon off the road. Hugh Dalton, the former Labour Chancellor of the Exchequer, sagely noted in his private diary: 'If this boy ever comes to the throne . . . it will be a very different country and Commonwealth he will rule over.'

After a difficult year staying with their in-laws at Buckingham Palace, Balmoral and Sandringham, Clarence House at last became available. 'It was still a shambles,' said Parker, 'but it was got together very quickly, and they furnished it with a lot of their wedding presents. There was a very small staff. The Princess invited us all to lunch every day, and was obviously very happy. You could hear her singing around the house. We were there long enough to see what heaven it could have been.'

For Philip, it was heaven indeed. For the first time in his life, he not only had a home of his own, he was also master in it. 'I suppose I naturally filled the principal position,' he told one of his biographers, Basil Boothroyd. 'People would come to me and ask me what to do.' These were poignant words, spoken by a man about a golden interval in his life. For a few brief years, he was king of his own castle, not walking two steps behind his wife, not excluded by constitutional practice from a huge slice of her life, but quite simply the head of the household.

At Clarence House, Philip behaved like the plain-spoken naval officer he was, not a gilded royal. 'We all thought a lot of him,' recalled the footman John Gibson. 'There was no pomp and ceremony, he was very rough and ready, but very interested in the staff. He made sure that we were all comfortable and insisted that we all had writing desks with Clarence House notepaper. They'd been given a TV set by Mountbatten as a wedding present, an unusual thing in those days. He even gave us that for the staff room. And when he came back from trips, he'd go right round the house to speak to everybody, just like a naval officer getting back to his ship.

'One weekend, they were down at Windlesham Moor in Surrey and the old Duchess of Kent threw a party, to which Danny Kaye came. He took some snaps with his Polaroid camera and, as he left, gave a deep curtsey. "You fool!" said Philip. Then he called the staff into the drawing-room and told us, "Now it's time for you to have a drink too."

'He wasn't royal to us. I always felt the old Royal Family just played the part, but he didn't play a part at all. He and the Princess were extremely happy, very lovey-dovey. They'd hold hands and kiss when they greeted each other. In those days, he didn't bother with pyjamas and in the morning, after he'd washed and shaved, he'd put his head round the door and say, "Aren't you up yet, Lilibet?" He wasn't keen on luxurious things. My wife worked in the kitchen and he'd often ask for sausage and mash for his supper. Lager was his favourite tipple.

'I just don't believe all that stuff about him having other women. I've met many gentlemen, you do in private service, and I had a feeling about some of them. He never gave me any other feeling than that he was devoted to her.'

Philip was certainly eager to convince Elizabeth that his footloose and fancy-free days were over. 'When we were moving his belongings into Clarence House,' recalled Gibson, 'we suddenly came across a lot of photographs. Some of them were of his old girlfriends before they married. "Good heavens!" he said. "Put those away." But she came in just at that moment and asked what we were doing. "Oh," he said, trying to pass it off, "just looking at old photos." "Not girlfriends, are they?" she asked. "No, no, Lilibet," he replied.'

For a profoundly shy girl who had come from a very sheltered home, it was a breath of fresh, salty air to be married to a husband who did not give a fig for protocol. 'I saw them when I was in Athens in 1950,' said a senior diplomat. 'Philip came into Piraeus on that funny little frigate *Magpie*, of which he had just been given command. She flew out to join him and they stayed with us in the embassy.

'Both my wife and I felt that he brought her out. She was very shy, rather withdrawn, a bit of a shrinking violet in fact, and he was young and vigorous and jollied her along. He didn't actually say, "Come on, old girl!" but it was that sort of thing.

'She was patently in love with him and responded. And he plainly felt great affection for her, though whether there was the same depth of love it's impossible to say. But I've no doubt that he had a very wholesome effect on her. He helped to make her what she's become. She is very shrewd but she had a protective shell around her, and he brought her out of it. We are extremely fortunate that he married her.'

The new Queen, with Margaret and the Gloucesters, at Badminton, April 1953, a few months before her coronation.

Their two years in Malta, where Philip had been posted as a First Lieutenant, were glory days for both of them. Elizabeth largely escaped the plod of duty, while Philip – particularly after he had been given his first command – was wholly absorbed by a job that he loved. For the first time in her life, Elizabeth was free to thoroughly enjoy herself, which was exactly what her father had hoped would happen. 'The King wanted her to be a normal officer's wife,' said Mike Parker, 'and told the Governor-General in Malta to soft-pedal the Princess bit. The result was that she only spent ten per cent of her time being one.'

As it happened, the Mountbattens were already in Malta – Lord Louis as commander of the First Cruiser Squadron of the Mediterranean Fleet – and Elizabeth and Philip went to live with them. Their home, Villa Guardamangia, sounded rather grand but was, in reality, a fairly modest place. 'My mother had to move out of her room, which was the best in the house, for the Princess,' said Lady Pamela Hicks, the Mountbattens' younger daughter, who had been one of Elizabeth's bridesmaids.

Elizabeth drove her own Daimler about the island, watched Philip playing polo, went on swimming expeditions with the Mountbattens and to all manner of parties. As she grew in confidence, the wallflower began to blossom. 'I remember one of the first parties they threw,' said Michael Parker. 'It happened on the quarter-deck of the ship, the girls were all going to be dressed up and the Princess asked me what she should wear. I told her that all the other girls would have simple cocktail dresses and no jewellery, so she shouldn't come in anything too pretentious. She said, "I've got just the thing," and turned up in a beautiful black dress. "Ma'am," I said, "that's a knockout!" She looked gorgeous and she knew it. She became quite coquettish, did a twirl and said, "Oh fiddle-de-dee!" Philip must have been very proud of her.'

Even in Malta, though, they were never lovey-dovey in public, 'She's not tremendously demonstrative,' said Pamela Hicks, 'and so, although they might hold hands walking in the garden, they'd never have spooned on a sofa. In those days, you didn't kiss in public, you really didn't. In any case, Philip is not the romantic Romeo, always rushing in with bunches of flowers, more the slightly overgrown schoolboy, a mixture of slightly prudish and very boisterous.'

Some of the naval parties were a good deal more exuberant than anything Elizabeth had been used to. 'I was with them while they were staying in Malta,' recalled Lady Henriette Abel Smith, then Elizabeth's lady-in-waiting, 'and there were some very wild parties indeed, with spoons and buns being thrown across the table, though luckily not butter. When the games became too boisterous, Philip would sit Princess Elizabeth on the piano with me to keep us out of the firing line.' Elizabeth showed no sign of missing her first baby, Prince Charles, who had been left with the nursery staff back in Britain. In fact, when she flew home from Malta for the first time, she went to a race meeting before going to see him at Sandringham, where he had been staying with his grandparents. The Queen was not maternal, let alone mumsy, even before she took on the burdens of queenship.

In April 1950, it was announced that she was to have a second child. She came back to England from Malta to have the baby, and Princess Anne was born at Clarence House in August of that year. Again, great crowds waited outside, hoping to catch a glimpse of her. This time, Elizabeth took longer to recover, but in November was well enough to fly back to Malta to spend Christmas with Philip. The two babies, meanwhile, were taken to Sandringham to stay with their grandparents. Again, hardly maternal.

The years in Malta were equally happy ones for Philip. Thus far, marriage had not forced him to give up his naval career, and the Navy fitted him like a glove. It met all his needs, psychological as well as physical. It gave him an outlet for his passionate desire to succeed. It allowed him to speak his mind even on the most formal occasions. 'When he was a First Lieutenant,' Lady Hicks recalled, 'he once had a complete blackout while he was doing a church service on board and forgot the words of the Lord's Prayer. But he just said, "Come on, you lot, you should be joining in!" – and got away with it.'

The Navy had also provided him with a surrogate family before he had one of his own. And it satisfied the wanderer in him, a habit which had been forced upon him in childhood and, by the end of the war, was so much part of his nature that he had become a sort of royal Odysseus. Early in 1946, he had written in a visitors' book in Australia: 'Whither the storm carries me, I go – a willing guest.' If he had roots, they were at sea.

'A ship was the most perfect place for him,' said Admiral Robert Woodard, who commanded the Royal Yacht *Britannia* from 1990 to 1995. 'It gives you an instant family and an amazing sense of security. It's a home. The number of Barnado's boys in the Navy is very high compared with the Army and the RAF. And Philip was a lonely soul, so capable and yet so utterly alone. His only real friends were his naval cronies. Command of a ship, when that comes to you, gives you a tremendous buzz.

You're the next thing to God. The C-in-C can be thousands of miles away. What you tell him is up to you. And you're responsible for the present and future of every man serving under you. It's exhilarating and gives you great freedom. The command of *Magpie* had all those ingredients for Philip.'

It was in the autumn of 1950 that Philip was promoted to Lieutenant Commander and given command of the frigate HMS *Magpie*. He proved to be a fiercely competitive and ambitious skipper, as the crew soon discovered. 'He wanted to be First Sea Lord,' said Mike Parker, 'and he'd have done it in spades. He was a *real* naval officer, twice as good as Dickie Mountbatten.'

Suddenly, their glory days in Malta vanished into thin air. In 1951, the King's grave illness made it obvious that Philip's naval career would have to come to an untimely end. His decision to retire from active naval appointments, says Parker, was very carefully thought through. 'No way was he told he *had* to leave. He wanted to help Elizabeth and knew that he couldn't do that if he stayed. There was a discussion and it became clear that he could not go on. The last night before we left Malta to go home was dreadful.'

Philip had consented to a brutal laceration of an essential part of his soul and spirit. He later became an Admiral of the Fleet but knew he had not earned it by his merits as a sailor. And, in his darker days at Buckingham Palace, of which there were to be all too many, he had to watch other men, often lesser men, climb the ladder of the Navy List, command what he might have commanded. 'Think of it,' said Woodard, 'a man who could easily have been Chief of the Defence Staff. To swap that for a yard behind the Throne!'

'Can you imagine,' said Philip's cousin, Lady Mountbatten, 'what it must have cost a rising young star like him to leave his profession for ever when he was still only in his late twenties?' Philip might not be touchy-feely, as Princess Diana was; he could nonetheless feel deeply disappointed.

That, moreover, was only the beginning of the sacrifices which were to be expected of him. On the last, bitterly cold day of January 1952, he and Elizabeth set off on an official tour scheduled to take them to Australia via Kenya. They were going in place of the King and Queen, since George VI was plainly seriously ill. Indeed, the young couple only set out after the King's doctors had announced, the day before their departure, that they were very well satisfied with his condition. The King was, at least, well enough to wave his daughter farewell at Heathrow.

Six days later, while Philip and Elizabeth were still in Kenya, the King died in his sleep and Elizabeth, at the age of only 25, was Queen. Both she and her husband were shattered, though for different reasons. 'When I told him,' said Michael Parker, 'he looked absolutely flattened, as if the world had collapsed on him. He had literally taken a king-hit. He saw immediately that the idyll of his life and their life together had come to an end. Elizabeth, of course, was also devastated by the news. Both then, and later on the plane taking us home, she was weeping inside and out. He was like the Rock of Gibraltar, comforting her as best he could.'

Martin Charteris, her private secretary, had already asked her what she would call herself. 'My name, of course,' she replied. 'What else?' She was proclaimed Queen Elizabeth II on 8 February. She was now married not only to Philip but also to those infinitely more demanding spouses, Britain, the Commonwealth and the Empire.

Parker hoped that she and Philip would at least be allowed to keep Clarence House as their home and use Buckingham Palace as an office. To him, the Palace seemed 'the coldest, more unfriendly, most unsatisfying place for any family to live in'. The new Queen was delighted with his proposal, but Churchill was not having it. 'Buckingham Palace was the centre of the Empire, where the Royal Standard flew,' said Parker. 'It came down heavy from the government that we *had* to move there. Elizabeth asked us to go with her for the short ride from Clarence House, and I can tell you there was not a dry eye in the car.'

Philip and Elizabeth's relationship, and their world, had been turned on its head. She was suddenly in a job – and what a job! – while he was out of one. Her work, as they both knew, would not only absorb by far the greater part of her time and energy, she would also be surrounded by a group of older men many of whom were hostile to and suspicious of her husband. 'The Court was against him,' said Lady Hicks, 'his mother-in-law was certainly very much against him and the Prime Minister, Winston Churchill, was against him.

'Like the Queen Mother, Churchill didn't like the Huns and he didn't like the nephew of the man who, so far as he was concerned, had given away India. Don't forget that the Queen was only in her mid-twenties, she had this world-famous Prime Minister, she was absolutely overwhelmed by him, and she was going to be directed by him in everything. No wonder Philip was knocked sideways.'

Elizabeth's Coronation took place in Westminster Abbey on 2 June 1953, the same day on which the world learned that Hillary and Tenzing had climbed Everest for the first time. Cecil Beaton, watching her enter the Abbey, said that despite her

splendid robes and Victorian diadem of precious stones, she still looked like a young girl, with a demeanour of simplicity and humility.

Philip, however, did not walk with her down the aisle. 'At the Coronation,' recalled Lord Charteris, 'Philip was in the procession, not beside her, as her mother had been with King George at his coronation. That was very much the advice of Tommy Lascelles, her new private secretary, who was bored by Philip. It looked *awful*. When they shouted *vivat, vivat, Regina*, she was on her own. Philip was just the first to pay homage to her. It was not calculated to make him feel cheerful!'

After the Oath and Holy Communion, Elizabeth shed all her robes and adornments and put on a white dress for the act of anointing, which took place out of the view of the television cameras. The Archbishop of Canterbury, Geoffrey Fisher, made the sign of the Cross over her hands, breast and head and pronounced 'as Solomon was anointed King by Zadok the priest and Nathan the prophet, so be thou anointed, blessed and consecrated Queen over the peoples whom the Lord thy God hath given thee to rule and govern.' Elizabeth, the thirty-eighth monarch of England in direct line from Egbert, who had become its King in the year 827, was the new Queen.

Even at home, where Philip had been the acknowledged head of the household, to whom everyone turned for decisions, the Queen was now the only one whom courtiers felt required to consult. The man who had always been accustomed to lead would always, from henceforth, be required to follow – in public at least. Philip had lost both his life and, to a large extent, his wife.

For Elizabeth, this posed almost as many problems as it did for Philip. How could she help this driven man, this fireball of masculine energy, to find a new and satisfying role, and in a world where her courtiers would have preferred him to remain silent and discreet?

From that moment on, as she knew very well, he would almost certainly become a volcano of frustration. Instead of merely being exuberant, as he had been in their early years, he would become ever more caustic as that frustration raged inside him. And then there was that other problem, her mother – now the Queen Mother – who, like Philip, was also out of a job and utterly bereft because of the loss of her husband. Elizabeth's family were to cause her more problems than the rest of her subjects put together.

Queen Elizabeth receives the homage of her husband at her coronation, Westminster Abbey, 2 June 1953.

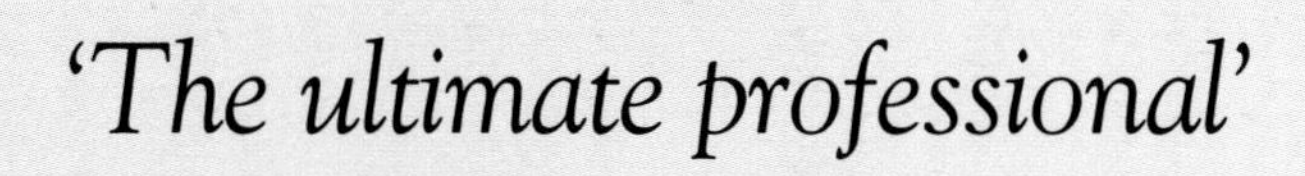
'The ultimate professional'

3 Her Majesty the Queen

The extraordinary thing, given that she was a young woman of twenty-six who had just had her life turned upside down, was that Elizabeth took to the job of being Queen like a duck to water. She may have been poorly educated in any formal sense – a mere seven and a half hours each week with her governess, Marion Crawford, plus twice-weekly lessons on Britain's constitutional history from the Vice-Provost of Eton, Henry Marten – but, from very early in her life, a sense of duty was as much part of her being as red and white corpuscles.

The King and Queen had certainly tried to prepare her for her future role by, among other things, making sure that she was present whenever they had important visitors for lunch or dinner – politicians, ambassadors, war leaders. Her mother always encouraged Elizabeth to talk to them. Eleanor Roosevelt, the wife of the American President, came away from Buckingham Palace thinking that the young Princess was not only serious but had a great deal of character and personality. She had also learnt to speak French fluently with the help of a Belgian aristocrat called Antoinette de Bellaigne.

Elizabeth had been made a Counsellor of State when she was only eighteen, which meant that she sometimes had to take the place of her father if he was away. Once, while he was visiting the Eighth Army in Italy, she had to sign a reprieve for a murderer. Fulfilling routine royal duties seemed to come to her naturally.

In the world of constitutional monarchy, continuity was what mattered. When she became Queen, she was not required to be innovative or indeed behave like a leader, other than by example. As her father had told her so often, 'Your job will be to take advice,' and that, given her lack of experience, she was only too happy to comply with. Her instinct, in any case, was to do things exactly as they had been done before, to follow the existing rules. As Philip once drily remarked, 'If it was customary to have porridge at every meal, Lilibet would have it.' As a result, the transition was a remarkably seamless one.

'From the beginning,' said Sir Edward Ford, her assistant private secretary from 1952 to 1967, 'I never felt she was diffident. She had extraordinary self-confidence really. Four years in Malta mixing with sailors helped. I don't think we ever felt she was nervous. She had extraordinary charm and a perfectly natural bravery. I never saw her scared in any way. On one of her early visits to Belfast, some madman dropped a paving-stone on to her car, but she just drove on as if nothing had happened. I was in the car behind, so I saw it all.'

Her courtiers also loved the fact that she was utterly predictable, that she positively relished routine, slipped into it as if it were her favourite day dress. 'The Queen is really a bureaucrat's dream,' Ford went on. 'She was wonderful to work for, always so accessible. She used to send for her private secretaries day by day and always at the same time – 10.30. We might have been her hairdresser. King George, whom I'd worked for previously, didn't like to be disturbed but she wasn't like that at all. You could press the button to her page at any time – "the President of X has died, should we send a telegram?" – that sort of thing.'

More surprisingly, Elizabeth does not seem to have wasted time in finding out what Philip thought. 'Except for big tours and speeches, she didn't depend on him,' said Ford. 'Things were not delayed so she could ask him. Right from the outset, she was very clear in her own opinions. Again, that was quite different from her father, who often used to squirrel things away so that he could ask Queen Elizabeth what she felt.

'And nothing, but *nothing* deflected her from duty. She'd go into labour and have a baby, so we knew we weren't going to see her for a while. But, within a very short time, twenty-four or forty-eight hours at most, she'd be asking whether there were any papers and would we care to send them up? The delay was minimal and they'd always be done the next morning. Sir Godfrey Agnew, who was Clerk to the Privy Council, used to say, "If only I got such speedy replies from Whitehall!"'

It was not as if documents of State arrived at the Palace in a dribble. They came in a positive deluge every single working day. There were red boxes stuffed with them from Number Ten, the Cabinet Office, the Ministry of Defence and, *in excelsis*, the Foreign Office – between twenty and fifty telegrams twice a day from all over the world. Everything her private secretaries winnowed out of this tidal wave of paper Elizabeth felt duty-bound to take aboard because she needed to be informed enough to deal intelligently with both her own ministers and officials and with officials from foreign and Commonwealth countries. Any other monarch might have found it a wearisome chore. On the contrary, Elizabeth seemed to find much of it absorbing, even though she had to spend two or three hours every day reading the stuff. She took pride in knowing the score well enough to keep even some of her Prime Ministers up to the mark. For example, she caught out Harold Wilson at his first audience with her, because she had picked up something which had escaped his attention. The result of this discipline over fifty years is that no British monarch has ever been better informed.

Despite the red boxes and all her other duties – State visits, foreign tours, days on official visits and openings all over Britain, investitures and audiences of all kinds – her private secretaries found dealing with her every morning thoroughly congenial. 'You talked with her as you might talk to a friend who was staying for the weekend,' said Ford, 'or in the way a husband and wife might sort out their day's engagements. "The Prime Minister is delayed, shall we put it off till tomorrow? What would you like to do?" The whole conduct of affairs was very informal and relaxed, far more so than it had been with the King.'

Nor, so far as her senior courtiers were concerned, was it any disadvantage that she was a woman, and a nubile, attractive one at that. Martin Charteris, the other assistant private secretary, was very starry-eyed about her, as everyone knew. 'I remember him kissing the newspaper with her picture in it,' recalled Lady Henriette Abel Smith. ' "I love her, I love her!" he cried.' Edward Ford felt much the same about a woman who did not hesitate to use her charms discreetly on these susceptible males. 'We were all slightly in love with her,' he said. 'She was

reserved but she could give you not quite a come-hither look, but one which was so friendly as to be encouraging. She made us feel like men.'

As the years went by, the more confident of her advisers would even take the risk of teasing her; and she, as one recalled, 'would respond slightly flirtatiously, once even measuring her hand against mine. There was another occasion when she'd been seeing off some State visitor at the Grand Entrance of Buckingham Palace. Afterwards, she stopped and chatted to half a dozen of us and I said something slightly teasing. She lifted up her foot to stamp on my highly polished toecap and said, "If you go on like that, I'll tread on your foot!" From the look I got from some of my colleagues, it was obvious they thought I'd sinned against the Holy Ghost!'

To those closest to her, it was obvious that she loved being Queen. 'She's been doing that job for half a century now,' said Ford, 'and I think she'd be miserable without it. She enjoys it in the same sense that I enjoy a hot bath. She gets her satisfaction in life from doing it. I never saw her complain about an engagement, never heard her say, "Oh God, another investiture!" or anything like it.'

There are, in point of fact, certain kinds of engagement which she contemplates with considerably less relish than others. 'She's not a whinger,' said one of her ladies-in-waiting, 'but I have heard her say, "Why are we going to another hospital?" The plain truth is that she's not as good with sick people as she is with the non-sick. Being so hugely strong herself, it's hard for her to empathize with them and, like the late Queen Mother, she prefers people who are very, very healthy.' She does not even have much time for members of her own family who are not well. 'With the Queen,' said a regular weekend guest at Sandringham, 'you're just not allowed to be ill. When we were there and Princess Margaret had clearly had one of the little strokes she had in the years before she died, the Queen just said, "She'd had another of her little turns." You're not supposed to have a stroke, you're expected to keep going.'

Any event which involves four-legged creatures is very much to her taste, but she is markedly unenthusiastic about two-legged sports. 'The Commonwealth Games came to Edinburgh in 1986,' recalled Sir Kenneth Scott, then an assistant private secretary at the Palace, 'and I fixed up a varied programme of events for the Queen, including weight-lifting, which had amused her at a previous games in Sydney. There was also a lot of athletics, because that's what I enjoy

Queen Elizabeth after her coronation.

myself! As we were setting out from Holyrood one day, the Queen murmured, "Is it athletics *again?*" So I said, "You could pretend they were horses, Ma'am" – and she laughed.'

Although far from being prey to vanity, she also gets irritated when courtiers do not allow her time for even the minimum of female refurbishment. On one particularly busy day in the 1990s, the Queen had had to take more time than usual to read her red boxes, with the result that her daily hair-do had been cancelled. As she was leaving Buckingham Palace for her eighth engagement, she spotted the man she held responsible, her private secretary, Sir Robert Fellowes, and complained: 'I really think I'm going to have to employ a woman!'

She loses her temper so infrequently that, when she does, it comes as a considerable shock to those who observe it. 'We were waiting in the drawing-room at Balmoral for the Queen's arrival,' recalled a senior civil servant. 'The conversation was a bit stilted but, when she eventually came in, she was smiling. Then, suddenly, she let rip and launched into a tirade which, we discovered, was directed at her then private secretary Philip Moore and one of the ladies-in-waiting.

'Her annoyance, not to say fury, arose from the fact that Princess Margaret, who was in London, had been asked to buy a new sweater for her and send it up to Scotland. But when the parcel had arrived the first time, it had been sent straight back to Buckingham Palace to be scanned because, at that point, they had no security equipment to do it in Balmoral. The box had only come back again from London that evening. When the Queen discovered what had happened, she flew into a rage and it really shocked me, because she was normally so controlled. What made it particularly unnerving was that, as she let rip, the smile which she'd had on her face when she first came into the room kept reappearing as she desperately tried to regain control of herself. The whole thing went on for two or three minutes. It was quite an eye-opener.'

The Queen has learnt from her father, who had an explosive and alarming temper, that disapproval from a monarch is multiplied a thousand times in the mind of either a subject or a royal servant. 'A mild rebuke from her,' said a former courtier, 'is like a knife in the guts. A dressing-down is close to death.' Her rebukes tend to be correspondingly gentle.

In November 1988 she decided that she would like to attend the opening of the Wightman Cup tennis match against the United States at the Royal Albert Hall. 'I went along to do the standard recce,' recalled Kenneth Scott, 'but, since it was a tennis match, I assumed that everybody would be dressed fairly informally. I didn't think it was necessary to ask what the royal party would be expected to wear. So the Queen went in a day dress and the men in the royal party wore lounge suits. Of course, when we arrived, we found that everybody else in the hall was in full fig – the men in dinner jackets, the women in evening gowns – no doubt because they knew the Queen was coming.

'At that point, the Queen made no comment but, at the end, as we were going out, she said very quietly to me, "I felt a little underdressed, didn't you?" If you've made an error of which she is aware, you'll know all right, but she doesn't dress you down – no pun intended! Nor,' added Scott, who had previously been the British Ambassador in Yugoslavia, 'would she ever say, "Mr X told me differently about that," because a quibble from a sovereign is devastating to the hearer.' That is why she has developed her own form of judgement-free, unemotional understatement. The question, 'Are you sure?' is Queen-speak for 'Good heavens, no!' The question, 'How would that help?' means, 'I think that's a rotten idea,' or, in a more relaxed Commonwealth setting, 'Forget it, sunshine!'

When her own judgement falters, on the other hand, the Queen is only too ready to acknowledge her errors. After the Lockerbie disaster in 1989, she decided – against the advice of Robert Fellowes – not to go to the site of the crash immediately, partly because she thought she would be in the way, partly because she has a horror of ambulance-chasing. Prince Andrew went in her stead. A fortnight later, she came up to Fellowes while he was with several other people and said, 'You were right about Lockerbie and I was wrong. I wish I'd gone there earlier.'

Under the sort of pressures she often faces, it is hardly surprising that she sometimes looks burdened. 'She came to the wedding of "Stoker" Hartington, the Duke of Devonshire's son,' recalled one of the Queen Mother's ladies-in-waiting, 'and afterwards I was standing with her in the hall. She was looking very serious, and then suddenly said, "Oh, I really must snap out of this and look smiley! I've had a whole morning full of problems."'

If she is landed with what she regards as a bizarre engagement during a State visit abroad, as she was in Italy in 2000, she will murmur behind her hand, 'Why am I here?' On that occasion, when an aide explained that the Italian government had thought it a good idea, she simply said, 'Yuk!' If the event is merely mind-bogglingly boring, on the other hand, her *ennui* remains unspoken. In York two years ago, I saw her standing stolidly in a marquee watching youngsters giving

an inept display of mime as the rain poured down outside. Why, I thought, is she asked to do such things? By then, after all, she was well into her seventies.

Her dedication and consistency are well-nigh superhuman. No head of state in the world can match her devotion to duty, still less the efficiency with which she has done her job for half a century. She is the ultimate professional. In the whole course of British history, we have never had a more unfailingly dutiful monarch. She wins no prizes for imagination, charisma or small talk but, if a panel of learned historians were giving awards for the most reliable, unflappable, biddable and least complaining monarch in our history, she would sweep the board. And she does not even think of herself as dutiful.

A senior civil servant who went to Balmoral in 1979 with Mrs Thatcher for the first of the Prime Minister's annual visits was amazed to see the Queen dealing with correspondence as soon as dinner was over. 'When the meal had been cleared away,' he recalled, 'she brought in a huge basket of letters from the public, many of them about the murder of Lord Mountbatten in Ireland, which had just happened. She was plainly more interested in reading them than in making small talk.'

That, moreover, is simply par for the course. 'When she is supposed to be on holiday at Sandringham or Balmoral,' said Kenneth Scott, 'almost every day the private secretary on duty will take her a great big basket full of papers which have to be read and signed. When she is going to Windsor for the weekend, we send her another large box of papers and, by the following Monday, they invariably come back dealt with and, where necessary, annotated with instructions as to what we're to do. She never hangs on to paper.'

There are precious few moments at either Sandringham or Balmoral which are entirely free of either problems or visitors. For example, the arrival of Paul Keating, the Australian Labour Prime Minister, at Balmoral in 1993 was scarcely a vacation-enhancing event. The Queen had already met him on a visit to Australia in the previous year and knew that he and his party were committed to turning the country into a republic by 2001. Keating, moreover, had been the 'villain' of the infamous *noli me tangere* episode, when he was ludicrously accused by some newspapers of having touched the royal person at a reception.

Queen Elizabeth in 1958, wading into one of the tide of red boxes.

Keating says that he does not know whether he actually touched the Queen's back or not, that all he was trying to do was make sure she knew some of the people there and, to that end, was steering her towards Dame Pattie Menzies, widow of the former Australian Prime Minister. 'When the tabloids started screaming about it,' Keating recalled, 'she said to me, "You must take no notice of them." I replied, "You may be surprised, Ma'am, but I'm not."'

When Keating and his wife arrived in Britain the following year, the Queen knew that, however courteous they might be to each other, the issues they had to address were going to be thoroughly uncongenial to her. So, in the days before Keating turned up at Balmoral, there were somewhat fraught discussions about how best to handle him. 'Before he came,' recalled Kenneth Scott, 'we talked about whether we should give him a barbecue supper – which the Queen thought he might find patronizing – or a formal dinner, black tie, with bagpipes afterwards. I thought that might prove rather sticky, so we settled on a barbecue to be cooked by Prince Philip. In the end, I had the sense that Keating *did* feel a bit patronized, but maybe she couldn't have won either way. Later on in the weekend, they had an hour's audience in the Queen's sitting-room.'

Keating remembers thoroughly enjoying the barbecue, but the Queen certainly did not enjoy the audience. 'I told her,' said Keating, 'that, although no reflection on her, it was no longer appropriate for our head of state to be the British monarch, and that in no way could the monarchy continue to represent the aspirations of Australians. She replied that she had always been conscientious about visiting and dealing with Australia and that her only wish was to do what the Australian people wanted her to do.'

The Queen plainly found the conversation extremely hard going. 'I've no doubt they were frightfully polite to each other,' said Kenneth Scott, 'but she clearly hadn't found him at all sympathetic and, when she came out, she said, "Now I really do need a very large drink." And she had a whopping dry Martini.' So much for 'holiday' visitors.

Not only is the Queen always available, even when supposedly taking a break, she is always ready to listen to, and accept, advice. One of her recently retired private secretaries says that 'On the topics I was dealing with, which included major overseas trips, the Queen would take my advice ninety-five per cent of the time. Occasionally, she'd sniff a problem and query something – and, in my experience, she was never wrong to query. On ceremonial or military things, though, I'd always ask *her* advice.'

Sometimes, particularly where an issue has political connotations, she will accept advice even when it goes against her own instinct. 'Before we went to Ethiopia in 1965,' said Sir Edward Ford, 'our Ambassador there, Sir John Russell, and the Governor of Eritrea, who was a cousin of the emperor, Haile Selassie, told me that they were very keen that the Queen should give back to the Emperor the Ethiopian royal insignia, which General Sir Robert Napier had captured – stolen really – at the Battle of Magdala in 1868, when he rescued some British diplomats. There was a hat, rather like a Doge's cap, and a sceptre, but they were the equivalent of the Crown Jewels to them. They had been kept in a case in the Armoury at Windsor Castle.

'I was tickled by the idea, but the Queen was rather reluctant. Eventually, she said, "All right, you can take them out there and we'll see how the visit goes." It went very well and, when it came to the final banquet in Asmara, where the Queen was to make the final speech, she agreed that we should give the insignia back. Bennett, the Queen's page, went ahead of us to the room where the banquet was to be held, and hid, along with the insignia, behind a curtain. He was told to produce them at the critical moment and lay them before the Emperor.

'Everything worked according to plan. Haile Selassie was a very black man but, when the insignia were presented to him, he went green with emotion. He actually changed colour, he was so deeply moved. I was almost in tears myself. But the Queen was right. It was a mistake. I don't know where those things are now, with all that's happened in Ethiopia. If you pressed her to do something, she'd do it but, as in this case, she often had a sort of instinct that it was not wise.'

The Queen's readiness to accept advice from her ministers has occasionally landed her in some very embarrassing situations. Her decision to allow Sir Anthony Blunt, her Surveyor of Pictures, to remain a member of the royal household after he had been unmasked by MI5 as a KGB agent in 1964 still puzzles and dismays some of her most senior former advisers.

'I think I know what happened,' said a man who was a senior courtier at the time. 'The Permanent Secretary at the Home Office, Sir Charles Cunningham, came to see Sir Michael Adeane who was then the Queen's private secretary, at the Palace and told him what MI5 had discovered, but said that we didn't want to "out" Blunt because he might still have useful information to give us. It's inconceivable that Adeane didn't tell the Queen. He didn't, though, tell any of us. He was an absolute clam.

'I'd have thought she would initially have said, "I can't have a known spy as

a member of my household, it'll eventually become known and people will ask why I kept him on even though I knew." But if she'd then been strongly advised to let him remain in his post, she'd have complied. The Queen Mother, whose judgement was usually less good, wouldn't have worn it for a moment, but the Queen did.'

'I do think it was an error,' said one of the Queen's former advisers, who was working in the Palace when the story finally broke. 'I still find it astonishing that Adeane would have advised her to keep him on, and that she accepted the recommendation. It says a great deal about the matter-of-factness of the woman, but she plainly felt that, if that was what ministers wanted, she was constitutionally bound to accept their advice.

'I'm also amazed that the decision to keep Blunt didn't do the monarchy more damage when the facts eventually became public in 1979. I do know that we spun it with great difficulty. Our spin of course was that it had been a constitutional requirement, that the Queen had felt obliged to do what ministers asked her to do, but I'm astonished that we got away with it so lightly in public relations terms.'

'I once asked the Queen whether she *had* been told about Blunt,' recalled a retired mandarin. ' "D'you know," she replied, "I just can't remember whether they told me or not" – and I don't think she was dissembling. Then she added: "I find that I can often put things out of my mind which are disagreeable."' Even her memory serves the constitution. 'I can't think of anyone else who could forget that she had been told,' said one of her former private secretaries, 'but *she* could.' Her ability to put unpleasant facts out of her mind also, in some measure, explains how she managed to weather the years when almost her entire family became a marital disaster area.

The one thing which the Queen most obviously lacks in her public appearances is what one veteran courtier calls 'outward humanity', a quality which Princess Diana had (and Prince Charles has) in spades. Watching her and Prince Philip on their visit to York in 2000, it struck me that wherever Philip went among the crowd, there was laughter. Where the Queen went, there was very little indeed. She simply does not have his gift for reaching out to strangers. She is neither touchy nor feely.

'I remember being in Iran with her in the days of the Shah and his wife Farah Diba,' said one of her former

The Queen's 1953 Christmas broadcast to the Commonwealth from Auckland, New Zealand.

aides, 'and we visited a school for blind children with them. The children came running and the Queen was very nice, but Farah instinctively went and hugged them. I'm sure the Queen had the same sentiments but she could not bring herself to do the same thing. I did see her touch lepers in Nigeria in 1956 but it wasn't what you would call wholehearted.'

'There has been a slow change in her behaviour since Diana died,' observed a veteran lady-in-waiting, 'but even now she would never take a baby on her knee or sit on a hospital bed. There is still a tremendous buttoned-up-ness. I was with her in Belgium in the 1960s just after Queen Fabiola and King Baudouin had married. Fabiola was dressed entirely in white and, when a blind child came on the scene as she was about to meet the Queen, she immediately bent down to the ground and put her hands on its face. She could easily have dirtied her dress in doing so, but that didn't seem to cross her mind. The Queen would *never* do a thing like that.'

There is no doubt that the Queen is buttoned-up when it comes to public appearances. Deep in her bones is a sense that monarchy must keep a certain distance if it is to retain any sense of magic. That instinct has nothing to do with snobbery of any kind. In many ways, indeed, the Queen is a strikingly humble woman. She very rarely says 'I' and, unlike Princess Diana, conveys no sense that she wants to be the centre of attention. 'Driving with her through the middle of that huge island at Hyde Park Corner, something only she is allowed to do,' said one of her most senior ladies-in-waiting, 'I said, "It's still a thrill to do this." "Oh, do you think so," the Queen replied, "but it's so conspicuous." If you are essentially a shy, retiring character, as she is, you don't want to be to the fore.'

'I thought it was bloody marvellous to be able to go through that gate and under the arch,' said a former senior courtier who still sees a good deal of the Royal Family, 'but the Queen can't bear to be thought to be showing off. She equates that kind of thing with abuse of privilege, which is the weakness of most world leaders. We and the police had to work on her for almost twenty years to persuade her to have motor cycle escorts. "I can't have all those sirens blaring," she'd say, "I'd be like Idi Amin or Gadaffi."'

'With too many members of the Royal Family,' said one of the Queen's former private secretaries, 'arrogance is deeply ingrained in their natures, but not in hers. She is the very opposite of self-important, in fact I've never known anyone who was less self-absorbed. It is very odd to watch her sidle into a room.

She doesn't ever try to make an entrance. The Queen Mother always did and then everybody burst into applause, as the old lady intended. The Queen couldn't be more different. So many times I've seen her slide into a theatre or cinema seat in a way which made it clear that she wants to be as little obvious as possible. It was just the same when she went into the royal box at Covent Garden. She always sat down quickly rather than milk the applause.'

Nor does she always stand on her dignity when someone fails to keep an appointment. 'Normally I went to see her on a Sunday evening,' recalled a former incumbent at the Royal Chapel in Windsor Great Park. 'Once, though, I fixed a date for Saturday instead, but then totally forgot that I'd made the switch and turned up on Sunday as usual. The Queen didn't give me my normal glass of gin, but we spent twenty-five minutes together and she didn't say anything, so I thought no more about it.

'Then, when I came to file the correspondence, I saw that it said Saturday and realized I'd made a terrible blunder. I asked Robert Fellowes, who was then her private secretary, to apologize for me and, the following Sunday, told her that I had been covered with confusion. All she said was, "I thought *I'd* got it wrong." She didn't even get someone to ring and ask where I was.'

The Queen was similarly modest and accommodating when a former permanent under-secretary at the Foreign Office asked if he might be excused from having to go to the Palace to receive *every* new ambassador with the Queen. Since there are fifty new heads of mission each year, it is a considerable chore for the permanent under-secretary. 'You had to wear diplomatic uniform,' he recalled, 'and, since I kept mine at my tailors in Savile Row, I had to rush off there, get myself poured into it and then hurry back to the Palace. It took up half the morning. 'After I'd been permanent under-secretary for two years, I asked the then Lord Chamberlain if the Queen would mind if I sent my deputy, should I have a really important meeting. His response was wholly negative. Six months later, when I saw him again, I said, "I don't want to nag but, with a minor African country whose ambassador you might never see again . . ." "Ask her yourself," he replied. So, the next time I was alone with the Queen, I did and she simply said: "Of course! I'd never thought about it, but it must be an appalling chore for you while, for me, it's just part of a day's work." She was totally unpompous and understanding.'

Despite appearances – in public, she often looks as if she has just smelled something rather nasty – the Queen also has a rollicking sense of fun and an

acute sense of the ridiculous. Like any good politician, though, she knows that a sense of humour can be extremely dangerous and that she cannot be seen to laugh at other people, however bizarre their behaviour.

Early in her reign, there were occasions when she simply could not keep herself in check. 'I can remember a visit to Dover,' said Edward Ford. 'It was a place we hadn't been to for quite a few years. Unusually, we had a few minutes to spare before lunch, and the Queen found herself in the town hall with the mayor in his robe and chain. To pass the time, she went to look at a glass display case, which contained a magnificent mayoral chain with diamonds set in it. "That's very lovely," she said. "When do you wear it?" "Only on very special occasions," replied the mayor. At that, she just put her head back and roared with laughter.'

As the years went by, she learned how to contain herself, though it was often a near thing. 'I remember that we went to a small Welsh town in Silver Jubilee year,' recalled one of her ladies-in-waiting, 'and they'd brought together youngsters from the local schools to show off their musical talent. There was one girl of fifteen or sixteen who was a very good singer. She came forward, she had the most enormous bosom and she was holding a white handkerchief to it, as some singers do. Thinking the pianist was ready, she took a very deep breath and everything, including the bosom, went up. She held it for as long as she could but then noticed that the poor pianist had got all his music muddled, so everything had to come back down. When he finally sorted himself out, the girl took another enormous breath, and everything went up again. I thought the Queen was going to die. She looked at me and both of us almost cracked up.'

A visit to a small Scottish town which had a lady mayoress showed just how firm the royal control had become. 'Towards the end of the day,' recalled one of her aides, 'the Queen was invited to take tea on a broad sweeping lawn. She sat at a table with the lady mayoress and, in due course, a tray was brought out with a silver teapot. Then the lady mayoress turned to the Queen and said, "Now, Your Majesty, would you like to be mother, or shall I?" Two of the royal party burst out laughing and you could see the Queen swallow but she just said, "No, I think *you* could pour."'

The Queen making President Ronald Reagan laugh at a State Dinner in Washington, DC.

One thing she particularly enjoys is when some deeply solemn occasion is temporarily thrown into chaos. 'At my first Garter ceremony in St George's Chapel at Windsor, with all the great and the good there,' recalled one royal chaplain, 'the then Bishop of Winchester, Colin James, stood up to read the lesson. Perhaps the verger had assumed that it would be printed in the order of service but, when the bishop arrived at the lectern, he found there was no Bible there.

'So he said, rather pompously, "Would a member of this foundation kindly furnish me with a copy of the Holy Scriptures?" but nobody moved. So he said it again, rather more pointedly. You can never find a Bible in church, can you, so a minor canon had to slide out to get one – and then the service carried on. The following Sunday, when I saw her, I asked the Queen whether she'd had a good time at the Garter ceremony and how unfortunate it had been about the lesson. "Oh yes!" she said, eyes gleaming, "*wasn't* it fun?"'

'If someone makes a fool of themselves,' said one of the Queen's racing friends, 'she always finds it amusing. I remember being at a barbecue picnic at Balmoral. Prince Philip and Princess Anne were doing the barbecue and, when the Queen arrived, black smoke was still pouring out. She was thrilled that these great experts had clearly blundered. Instead of complaining that dinner was going to be late, she roared with laughter and said, "Made a complete hash of it, haven't they?"'

Since she can never express her real feelings in public, the Queen always has to wait until after the event. Then, when she has cast aside the official face which she has been wearing like a mask for most of the day, she will, as a former Master of the Household told me, 'mimic anyone and anything'. Admiral Woodard, in the course of his duties on board *Britannia*, has seen many of her impressions and is amazed how accurate they are. 'If you shut your eyes,' he said, 'she's as good as Rory Bremner.'

No one is exempt: the lord mayor of the city she has visited that day, the ambassador whose credentials she has just received, even her own Lord Chamberlain – all get the same treatment. Occasionally, though, she jumps the gun and the joke backfires. There is a story, almost certainly not apocryphal, about a Commonwealth diplomat who arrived at Buckingham Palace to present his credentials. The Queen thought he had left the room and began mimicking him. Then she noticed, to her consternation, that he was still standing by the door. 'Not bad, Ma'am,' he said graciously, 'not bad,' before bowing himself out.

She does celebrated imitations of Neil Kinnock and Boris Yeltsin, and is equally good on her own courtiers. Sir Sonny Ramphal, the former secretary-general of the Commonwealth, says that, when she was with him, she mainly mimicked politicians. Had she, I asked, ever mimicked Lady Thatcher? I won't answer that question,' replied Ramphal with a grin. Tony and Cherie Blair will certainly be part of her repertoire by this time; and her John Prescott would be well worth seeing.

'The Queen has a very acute ear,' said one of her ladies-in-waiting, 'and of all the people I've ever known, she is by far the most observant. If she were here with us, she'd remember – twelve years from now – that you came for tea wearing a Black Watch tie and a pink shirt. She'd say, "D'you remember the day we had tea together at Lady X's place?" and then take your voice off. I remember going country dancing with her in Edinburgh, and all those genteel ladies from Morningside were holding their dresses off the floor like this. Afterwards, she took them off perfectly and had us all rocking with laughter.'

'The whole thing,' remarked a Conservative peer who has often visited Balmoral and Sandringham, 'is based on the most acute observation of human foibles. You feel a powerful judge of character behind it. To be frank, it's a bit cruel to mimic some poor unfortunate in that way and, in a curious way, it is also cruel to be so mercilessly observant. But the Queen is conscious of the dangers and, if that is her way of relaxing and making a joke of what is, after all, a desperately formal life, then so be it.'

But why does she do it? 'It's partly a way of relieving the boredom,' explained a former courtier, 'and shattering the formality with which she is so hedged about. And then don't forget that her real self has been bottled up the whole day. This is her way of expressing it.' It is as if the real Elizabeth has been watching from behind her official self and cannot wait to have *her* say.

'With me,' said Sonny Ramphal, 'she usually used mimicry to reinforce something she'd been saying. It was a coded expression of opinion. She wasn't putting people down but conveying a message without actually putting it into words. It was, if you like, a pictorial nuance of her private opinion, and, at the same time, a way of giving fresh air and freedom to her real self.'

Senior politicians who have spent a good deal of time with the Queen believe they can spot the signs of that real Elizabeth showing herself. 'In private,' said Lord Hurd, the former Tory foreign secretary, 'she has a deep, rather masculine laugh, a fox-hunting sort of laugh. Her voice goes right down from its normal artificially high level to something really earthy. I think that's the real Queen. That laugh suggests to me that there is someone else down below.'

'The Queen swept here'

4 Elizabeth in Private

The Queen is a woman under both discipline and constraint. It is not often that she can really relax, say what she likes, do what comes naturally. There is, after all, something rather unnatural about having to resort to mimicry to express your true feelings and opinions. Even at home, she has to watch her tongue. There are always guests or royal servants to remark her every word.

They may be part of her trusted circle but, as she knows full well, what she has said is certain to be passed on within that circle, through the sly leak of gossip. It is the same old story: information spells power. Knowing what the Queen thinks, in that closed little world, marks out the *real* insider. Even at a graveside, courtiers will observe that she weeps, and wonder if they are tears of sorrow or tears of bitter anger for what the not-so-dear departed has cost her and her family. That, too, becomes the subject of speculation and gossip. Nothing she does or says, in public or in private, goes unnoticed and unremarked. She is always on the record.

Of course there are times, even with politicians present, when she literally kicks off her shoes and lets her hair down. That used to happen on *Britannia* more than anywhere else, because that was the one place – in blouse and slacks – when she felt truly on holiday. But, wherever it is, she is aware that lowering her guard carries a risk, that when she reveals, over a lunch table somewhere in the Commonwealth, that she takes the gloomiest view of the prospects for real peace in Ireland, it will somewhere enter the pool of insider knowledge. She takes that risk far more than she used to. She has, after all, been doing the job for a very long time, feels far more confident than she did in those early years and, anyway, it is impossible to remain permanently buttoned-up, twenty-four hours a day, especially after a couple of Martinis.

Hence, in part, her preference for the company of dogs and horses rather than human beings. That preference is patently obvious to all those who know her well. How astonishing, I once remarked to Edward Ford, that – after fifty years of State visits and walkabouts – the Queen should still be better at dealing with horses than with people. 'She's just as good with dogs,' he retorted drily.

Asked by a courtier thirty years ago what she missed most when she went abroad, she thought for a moment and then replied, 'The dogs.' For the Queen, remarked a veteran lady-in-waiting, it had always been dogs and horses first, even before her children. 'She talks to the dogs when you're there, but not to you,' complained one of the Queen Mother's ladies-in-waiting.

Courtiers who care nothing for either dogs or horses often feel thoroughly beached in the royal palaces. 'At Windsor weekends,' sighed one of the Queen's former advisers, recalling scores of mind-numbing conversations over lunch or dinner, 'there is no talk except about the horse. They ride it, race it, drive it and bang on about it incessantly from morning till night. If you know nothing and care even less about the horse, you're useless.

'At Buckingham Palace, thank God, the conversation is more about politics, but that's not to say there's no horse-talk even there. When I was in the Palace, Lord Carnarvon, who was then the Queen's racing manager, would ring up all the time to give her the latest racing news and John Miller, who was the Crown Equerry in charge of the Royal Mews, was always sidling upstairs with the latest from the Palace stables.'

The entire establishment seems to be festooned with horses – sixty racing and breeding horses at Newmarket, Marlborough, Beckhampton and Wolferton; thirty carriage horses at Buckingham Palace; innumerable breeding horses and ponies at Hampton Court; not to mention Prince Philip's carriage horses. Any free space closer to the ground is filled with a host of dogs: corgis, dorgies, cocker spaniels – Flash and Bisto are the Queen's current pair – and labradors, with Donna and Gem the field favourites at the moment.

If anyone, including herself, is bitten by one of her dogs, the Queen makes it abundantly plain that it is never the animal's fault, as one of Mrs Thatcher's aides discovered when he went to Balmoral with his boss. 'The Queen got very cross with me,' he recalled, 'because I trod on one of those damn dogs and it nipped me. There was absolutely zero sympathy. She made it clear that I was entirely to blame, that the dog was the injured party!'

He need not have felt put out. There was nothing personal about the Queen's rebuke. It was exactly the same when, in June 1981, a disturbed young man fired six blank cartridges towards her during the Trooping the Colour. When two cavalrymen converged on her to offer reassurance and protection, she told them brusquely to push off – the phrase she actually used was a good deal more pungent. 'Those two idiots came up behind me,' she complained to one of her staff later, 'and asked if I was all right. I said, "I was until you came – you're upsetting my horse!"'

In all this, of course, the Queen is little different from any number of other countrywomen. In her case, however, the fact that she is more at ease with animals has a far deeper significance than mere natural preference. For a woman who is so constantly surrounded by people that she scarcely knows what privacy is and, for half a century, has been the principal player in a seemingly endless round of ceremonial duties, it is not too much to say that her dogs and horses have helped keep her sane.

With them, this flawlessly, obsessively dutiful woman, who feels that she can never in public allow the mask of regality to slip, can be entirely herself. With them, she has no role to play, no dangerous, revealing words to stifle. 'She doesn't need to be guarded with the animals,' said a former private secretary. 'They're not going to repeat what she says, they won't even remember it, so they can be trusted.'

Dogs and horses, what is more, neither know nor care who she is. So, with them, all the trappings of monarchy and human expectation fall from her burdened shoulders and she becomes, for an hour or two, an ordinary woman. 'To a dog,' said Bill Meldrum, a long-serving gamekeeper at Sandringham, 'it doesn't matter whether you're the Queen or a down-and-out living on the streets of London. The Queen's dogs love her and nobody else, but not because she's Queen. And there's another thing. There are a lot of people round her who say what they think she wants to hear, but from the dogs she gets total honesty.'

The fact that they behave entirely naturally with her makes them a blessed relief from virtually the entire two-legged population of these islands. 'One of the Queen's greatest problems,' said the widow of a much-loved courtier, 'is that nobody except Prince Philip can be quite themselves when they are with her. The day you're natural with the Queen is the end of monarchy. If you were not to get butterflies in your stomach when you met her, she would just be an ordinary person. But how awful it must be when nobody can be themselves with you!' As a former courtier remarked: 'For her, animals are the natural world, people – all too often – the unnatural world.'

The Queen may sometimes look like a well-dressed middle-class mum, but the most surprising people seize up when they encounter her. 'I've been in her presence many times, at Buckingham Palace, Balmoral and Windsor,' said a senior civil servant who was private secretary to three Prime Ministers, 'but I've never had a proper conversation with her because I'm almost petrified – like a stuffed dummy, in fact.'

The formidable Lady Salisbury, who had known the Queen as a girl, came back from a visit to Windsor soon after her accession and told her family that she had been 'distinctly awed' by the Queen's obvious regality. One of Winston Churchill's family who is older than the Queen admitted to me that she found her 'quite frightening – she gives you a pretty good look if she thinks you're off the mark'. Even her favourite private secretary, Lord Charteris, that most unselfconscious of men, told me that he had never been able to forget that she was Queen.

The same goes even for regular shooting and

Queen Elizabeth with her favourite horse Betsy, at Sandringham in 1964.

stalking guests at Balmoral. 'There are times when I've been almost totally relaxed in her presence there,' said one, 'but, even then, you'd still be minding your Ps and Qs. She enjoys being teased but you'd hesitate to risk doing it. Can I get away with it? you'd wonder. You're always second-guessing yourself in that way, because it would be so *awful* if it went wrong. I once asked Philip Moore, then her private secretary, if he could ever forget that she was Queen and he replied: "Never, though you can get close after several whisky-and-sodas."' The most relaxed of her ladies-in-waiting, who has known the Queen as a friend for half a century, admitted that she only felt natural with her 'eighty-five per cent of the time'.

Even those who have been with her on holiday know that they must never take liberties. 'She's so quick to put you at your ease,' said Admiral Robert Woodard, 'that it's very easy to fall into the error of overfamiliarity. You then realize that you are beginning to treat her as a normal person, and that obviously can't be allowed. When I went over the top, her eyebrows would go up and I'd apologize. She hoped you would sort out the distance you needed to keep. Don't forget that her children bow whenever they come into a room where she is. The formality is totally inbred. Her dogs and horses have to fulfil the function of normality.'

They do even more than that. They provide a vital lightning conductor for her emotions, because she can express feelings about them with a freedom she seldom permits herself with people. Martin Charteris told me that he had written her a good many personal letters but had seldom received a reply. Yet, after his golden labrador Jessie had swallowed a poisoned egg which was intended to kill rats, and died as he and his wife Gay looked helplessly on, they received a flood of heartfelt letters from the Queen and several other members of the Royal Family.

Others have had precisely the same experience. 'The Queen is godmother to my eldest daughter who, at one point, fell desperately ill,' said a former lady-in-waiting. 'I was so distraught that I wrote to the Queen, but she never wrote back. Then, a few years ago, one of her corgis was killed in a fight with one of the Queen Mother's dogs, so I sent her my condolences and got a six-page letter by return of post! The feelings are all there but, because of the constraints of the Queen's life, they can't be expressed unless it's about an animal.'

Similarly, when Lord Mountbatten and one of his grandsons were murdered by the IRA, the Queen – astonishingly – did not write to the boy's mother, who had herself been wounded in the explosion, even though she is one of her closest friends. 'The Queen wouldn't write because she wouldn't want to become emotionally involved,' explained a veteran lady-in-waiting. 'When there's something she'd rather not face up to, she prefers to go for a walk with the dogs.' Perhaps we all feel a little like that at times.

The uninhibited side of the Queen, what Douglas Hurd calls 'the real Queen', blossoms whenever she is dealing with animals, and particularly dogs, which she handles extremely skilfully. When Bill Meldrum arrived at Sandringham in the early 1960s, he found that she was already a capable dog handler. With his help and regular training – for a time, they went out together every day – she became so expert that, as he says, 'She could put a dog on a sixpence at 500 yards with no problem.'

For several years, she took part in friendly dog trials at both Sandringham and Balmoral. 'In those trials,' recalled Meldrum, 'the judge would have a canvas dummy pheasant launched and then say to one of the handlers, "The dummy's a hundred yards out there, I want to see your dog hunting for it in that area." It's just like *One Man and His Dog*. You have a whistle round your neck and you blow it to either draw the dog back or drive it out further. You can be disqualified altogether for all manner of things. If the dog whines, for example, you're out.

'The Queen's not desperately competitive, but she won two or three times and came second on four other occasions. The last time she went in and won, she was down on her knees by the big scoreboard copying down all the scores, when two people came up. They didn't notice her because her back was turned, but she heard one of them say, "There's no doubt about which dog deserved to win today." She told me afterwards, "When I heard that, it made me feel really good, because it meant nothing had been pulled."'

The Queen has not run her dogs in trials for eight or nine years – 'She doesn't seem to have so much time,' said Meldrum – but she does still pick up dead and wounded birds on virtually all the shooting days at both Sandringham and Balmoral. 'She loves it so much she'd never miss it,' Meldrum told me, 'partly because it's something where she can compete with the best people in the country on equal terms. She's very good at it. As

a matter of fact, as a picker-up, she's worth paying.

'She does what any professional would do, stands three hundred yards behind the guns and spots where the birds fall. She'll work four dogs at the same time. Her cocker spaniels, Flash and Bisto – she calls them "the Hoovers" – sweep the nearer ground and she pushes her two labs, Donna and Gem, further out for the long-distance retrieves. A few years ago, at Balmoral, she brought off the finest retrieve I've ever seen.

'It was on the very last day of shooting and the Queen and I were together behind the line when this grouse was hit but flew on for quite a way before collapsing. I didn't see where it came down myself, but she has very good eyesight and saw that it had fallen on a peat hag about eight hundred yards away. "Have you a dog that can go that distance?" she asked me, but that day I hadn't taken my usual dog Sidney, so she sent hers, a black labrador bitch called Sherry.

'Now, she had to get the dog down the hillside and across one hundred and fifty or two hundred yards of dead ground, where she couldn't see her, then across a river which was about twenty yards wide and flowing fast. She stopped the dog before the dead ground, absolutely the right thing to do, shouted to her to get over and then shouted again to get her across the river.

'By that time, Sherry was on the far hillside five hundred yards away, with three hundred more still to do. The Queen told her on the whistle to keep going up the hill to the foot of the peat hag, which was three or four feet high with sheer sides. I thought she'd never get the dog up there at that distance, but she did – and immediately a grouse flew away.

'I said, "That's the bird." "No, it's not," she replied, "the one I want is dead and it's on the far end of the hag." She had to get the dog up there again on the whistle, but she did it, the dog picked up and brought the bird back. The whole thing must have taken ten or fifteen minutes. What the Queen and I didn't know was that, by this time, all the guns and beaters were watching, fifty or so of them altogether and, when Sherry came back with the bird, there was a burst of applause. The Queen said, "If I'd known you were all watching, I'd never have tried it!"'

Relaxing on Britannia *in 1977.*

The Queen's love of picking up, and the fact that she takes part in an activity which yields a great many wounded birds as well as dead ones, will strike many people as thoroughly gruesome. The shooting fraternity, however, like to point out that, in doing what she does with such skill, she is in some sense a sister of mercy amid the carnage.

'The pickers-up,' explained a regular guest at Balmoral, 'are the Florence Nightingales of the shooting field. Even the best shots wound birds terribly. The Queen takes infinite pains to find them and put them out of their misery. She carries a priest, which is a sort of miniature police baton with a weight at the end. When she gets a wounded bird, she hits it on the back of the head and it's dead in a trice. They're really humane killers. It's so much better than wringing necks.'

She responds to requests for her services on the shooting field with a thoroughly professional but somewhat unmonarchical meekness. 'She's given a map of where we'll be shooting each day and when we're likely to be at a particular place,' said Meldrum. 'At the bottom, I'd sometimes write, "Ma'am, we can do with you from the beginning today," meaning nine thirty. Mostly, she'd show up on time and say, "Meldrum said I was needed early."' In this, as in so many other ways, she is strikingly humble and biddable.

It is exactly the same when she goes racing. She may arrive at Ascot in a splendid procession of carriages down the course but, once there, affects no airs or graces. 'I was waiting for her to come one day,' recalled the man whose job it is to look after her while she is there, 'and she appeared at two o'clock as usual, smiling happily, but said immediately, "Why are you not in the paddock?" because she knew I had a horse of my own in the first race. She expected me to put the horse before her. It was as if she were saying, "Don't worry about me, I know the way."'

Indeed, she does: over the past half-century, the Queen has missed so few days of Royal Ascot that, by now, she knows the place as well as she knows Sandringham or Balmoral. 'Once, on Diamond Stakes day, she agreed to present the cup,' her racing aide went on. 'I knew that meant she had to get down to the unsaddling enclosure so, at what I judged to be the right moment, I said to her, "I think we ought to go down now, Ma'am." "Are you sure?" she replied. Very stupidly, I said, "Yes," with the result that we got down there seven minutes early. She had known *exactly* how long it would take. I said, "I'm really sorry for all the hanging around, Ma'am." She didn't say, "Well, I've been doing this for thirty-five years," just, "Never mind." Left to herself, she could run that racecourse perfectly well.'

The Queen has owned and bred horses for forty-nine years and knows all there is to know about equine pedigree. She inherited two thriving studs in Norfolk from her father. In 1972, she bought a third of Polhampton, where she keeps her yearlings; and, in 1982, acquired training stables at West Ilsley from Sir Michael Sobell and Lord Weinstock. 'If a sale is coming up,' said Sir Michael Oswald, manager and then director of the royal studs for twenty-nine years, 'you need to read the catalogue very carefully before you talk to the Queen. You mustn't miss any connection, even one that goes back as far as four or five generations, because *she* won't. She'll ask, "What do you think of Lot 268?" When you look at it, you'll see that the Queen bred the horse's great-grandam. If you fail to notice things like that, you don't score any brownie points.

'She also has a good deal to say about which stallion to send one of her brood mares to and which trainer to send a horse to. Some trainers suit a particular horse better than others. It's rather like deciding on schools for your children.' Lord Carnarvon, the Queen's late racing manager, once told me, 'Talking to her is almost like talking to a trainer.'

She spends around half a million a year on racing, all of it from what Oswald calls 'a very private purse, there isn't a penny of public money involved', but even that is a mere bagatelle in a world dominated by billionaire Arabs. Each of the four Makhtoum brothers has at least 200 brood mares and 300 horses in training. The Queen has around thirty of each. These days, she seldom buys new blood, because she simply cannot compete with their immense wealth.

The first newspaper she reads in the morning is the *Sporting Life*. Her racing manager and trainers can always get through to her on her private telephone numbers. Yet, sadly, she has precious little chance to see her horses actually race. 'Other owner-breeders at her level would get forty or fifty days' racing a year,' said Lord Carnarvon, 'and they'd be on the course to watch the vast majority of their horses run. The Queen only gets eight or ten days and she's lucky if she sees ten per cent of her horses race. For the most part, she has to watch them on tape in the evening. While she's doing other things, she's longing to know the result of the three twenty-five and

saying to herself, "Pray God they haven't forgotten to tape it!"'

Her observation of horses is just as acute as her observation of people. 'One day at Ascot,' her racing aide there recalled, 'I took her down to the paddock for the big race and, for some reason, neither of us had a race card. She looked at the horses and said what she thought of them. There was a very bright chestnut which particularly impressed her. She then went back to the Royal Box and after the race – which was won by a brightly coloured chestnut horse – I said, "That was the one you liked so much, Ma'am." "Certainly not", she replied, "it had one of those awful white plastic bridles." I hadn't noticed that as the horses flashed past, but she had.'

'I remember the Queen, when she was still Princess Elizabeth, sitting next to my father at polo matches when she and Philip were in Malta,' said Lady Hicks. 'A lot of the play always seemed to take place on the far side of the ground and, whereas my father would recognize the riders, the Queen always recognized the horses.'

Apart from her lifelong love affair with the horse, the Queen enjoys racing because, as with her dogs, she is competing on equal terms with other owner-breeders and because people who race tend to be a comparatively uninhibited crowd. 'There are fewer people in racing who are not themselves when they meet her,' explained her Ascot aide, 'and that is the way she likes it. On the course, she is not surrounded by heavies. If the police did that, they'd get very short shrift from her. The last thing she wants is for other racegoers to be inconvenienced. She regards the meeting as bigger than her. She is unbelievably modest.'

Guests at Sandringham and Balmoral are astonished at the menial tasks she undertakes herself when she is at home. 'I remember seeing her going round the house at Sandringham with a soda siphon and blotting paper mopping up after one of Prince Charles's incontinent puppies,' said one. 'She didn't ask anyone else to do it, though there were plenty of servants around.'

The Queen with obedient four-legged subjects, Balmoral 1967.

In some ways, indeed, the home life of our own dear Queen is rather less lofty than we might imagine. 'When you arrive at Sandringham or Balmoral,' said a lady who has stayed at both, 'she always shows you to your room herself and says, "I think you had this before." She does the seating for each meal in the main houses, where a lot of people with estates like hers would leave that to flunkeys. And, when you're having lunch or a candlelit dinner in one of the rather splendid log cabins in the grounds of both the estates, she'll lay the table herself. As a matter of fact, it's quite difficult to help her on occasions like that because everything has its place – she's rather obsessive in that way – and you're sure to get it wrong.'

'Then, during the meal,' said the lady's husband, 'the Queen comes round behind you and picks up your plate ready for the next course. Your natural instinct is to jump up and do it yourself. There's a terrible conflict between duty and pleasure, but she wouldn't want you to interfere. She much prefers to do it herself.'

'At the end of one meal,' his wife went on, 'I asked whether I could help clear up, but the Queen said, "No, thank you." The Royal Family always clean away and wash up afterwards, and the Queen doesn't really like people trying to help. There's a very set system and, unless you know exactly how it works, you're only going to be a nuisance.

'It's particularly difficult at the end of a meal. All the rubbish is put into a black polythene bag and, on one occasion, someone had tied it up before everything had been collected. "Who's done this?" the Queen asked, rather irritably, and untied it again. And if somebody puts a knife in the wrong box, they get a flea in their ear. The one thing you can safely do is pinch out the candles, which she insists must be used right down to the bottom. "There's still plenty of light in that," she'll say.'

Once, finding a shelter on the hill on the Balmoral estate in something of a mess, according to a courtier who was there, the Queen said, 'Let's clear this place up a bit,' and started brushing up herself. Sir William Heseltine, an Australian who was then her private secretary, quipped: 'Ma'am, I think we should put up a plaque saying, "Queen Elizabeth swept here," and she laughed.'

Visiting heads of state are given the same highly personal welcome. 'I didn't show them to their apartments,' said a former Master of the Royal Household, 'she and the Duke of Edinburgh did it themselves. The weekend before they came, she'd have gone through all the rooms they were going to use, pointing out that the light over a mirror wasn't quite right and so on.

The housekeeper would say to me, "The books have been changed, so I know the Queen's been here."'

At Windsor, too, she shows the same frugality as any cash-strapped housewife. 'One evening when we were all about to go to bed,' the former Master went on, 'the Queen looked from the private to the public side of the Castle and said, "All the lights are on, we'd better go and switch them off." So off we went together.

'The trouble was that a new-fangled system had been put in and, when we found the light switches, we discovered that, if you pushed the buttons hard, the lights came back on again and, if you just touched them softly, they merely faded. We eventually did get them all off, by which time the Queen was almost crying with laughter, because you didn't dare touch a button in case they all came on again. Then we had to find our way back in the pitch dark.' Again, the Queen did not think of telling someone else to do it.

The Queen's lack of loftiness no doubt owes something to a Christian faith, which enjoins the virtue of humility. 'It's not just a matter of duty for her,' said a former chaplain at Windsor, 'it's very much part of the fabric of her life. She loves Matins and the words of the Prayer Book have real meaning for her, though she was always ready to experiment with the old Rite A service if the Queen Mother was not around. Once, when there was no service at Sandringham, she went to Wolferton where they had children acting out the Gospel, and she found that rather fun. She only takes Communion three or four times a year, in the old Low Church tradition.'

'She prefers simplicity to pomposity,' said Kenneth Scott, 'so when she's at Windsor she'll go to the little chapel in the park rather than St George's, which she considers rather pompous. In Edinburgh, too, she doesn't go to St Giles. She prefers the Canongate Kirk where the minister, Charlie Robertson, makes her laugh. And there's always a pot of marmalade made by Mrs Robertson waiting for her at Holyrood.'

The Queen likes hymns with a good deal of thought in them – 'Dear Lord and Father of Mankind', 'Praise to the Holiest in the Height' and 'Glorious Things of Thee are Spoken' – no 'Kum Ba Yah's, thank you! – but she is not a great fan of sermons, particularly from visiting clerics who feel obliged to

sock it to her. 'She didn't want a chaplain on *Britannia*,' recalled Admiral Woodard. 'She told me, "I don't like sermons, you take the services." But she knows her Bible. Every Friday on the yacht, I'd go to the Queen with suggestions about readings and hymns and she'd quote the Bible without bothering to look it up. The prescribed reading might start at, say, verse nine but the Queen would say, "No, let's start at verse seven, otherwise it won't have the proper sense."'

A woman of routine in this as in everything else, she finds it rather strange if her ladies-in-waiting do not go to church regularly. 'She was very shocked that I'd skip church whenever I could,' said Lady Hicks, 'and that, when we were in Australia together, I'd prefer to go off riding on a sheep station on a Sunday morning. "Does she have a cold?" she'd ask when I wasn't at the service.'

On the other hand, she is not in any way puritanical. 'Shortly after I arrived on *Britannia*,' said another admiral who commanded the Royal Yacht, 'we suddenly discovered about six active homosexuals on the yacht and they had to go, because at that time it meant instant dismissal from the Navy and indeed the other Services. A couple of them eventually went to jail. I had to discuss it all with the Queen and was afraid it might prove embarrassing, but she just felt so sad for them. Several were long-serving yachtsmen. There wasn't a breath of puritanism in her attitude.

'But when, later on, I was at Buckingham Palace and one of her staff there was caught misbehaving with a housemaid – they were both married to other people – she was very disapproving indeed.'

More recently, it was discovered that a rather large quantity of gin – as much as a decanter a day – was disappearing from the Palace supply. The culprit turned out to be one of the Queen's own footmen, who confessed and was totally shattered. 'The Queen,' said a former senior courtier, 'was just deeply upset and said, "We must find him another job." He's now got one.'

She feels no need to copy the crowd of conformists who instantly distance themselves from anyone they feel has been tainted by scandal. In 1994, she went to distribute the Royal Maundy in Truro, where Michael Ball was the Anglican bishop. Ball's twin brother, Peter, had been Bishop of Gloucester until he resigned in 1993 after

Enjoying a quiet moment with her corgis in Windsor Park.

an allegation of sexual indiscretion. Peter Ball, however, had also been invited by Buckingham Palace to the lunch after the Maundy had been distributed, partly because he had previously preached a sermon at Sandringham which the Queen thoroughly enjoyed. Nevertheless, he made enquiries at the Palace to make doubly sure that his presence at the lunch would not be an embarrassment to the Queen. She replied that she would be disappointed if he were *not* there. At the end of the lunch, which was held in the chapter house, the Queen – who had been at high table with local dignitaries – broke away from the procession and went across to where Peter Ball was standing at a side table.

She held out her hand and said simply, 'My love and support, Bishop,' in the clearest of voices. Three of the people who heard it wept at the graciousness of what the Queen had done. One of them, who tells the story, says it was the best moment of the whole day. Both then and later, she has been a great deal more generous to Ball than some of his so-called liberal episcopal colleagues, who still object to him accepting invitations to take services in their dioceses.

The Queen has strong and well-informed views about many of her bishops and archbishops. She thought Michael Ramsay 'pretty stupid', according to Martin Charteris; liked Donald Coggan – 'straightforward, honourable chap, muscular Christian, no nonsense'; became fond of Robert Runcie (a former Scots Guardsman), after some hesitation; and, initially, was not overly taken by George Carey, who struck her as too much of a bare moralist.

For some time, she felt that he was always telling off the younger members of her family for being naughty boys and girls. The fact that she shared his view entirely still left her wishing that he would temper his morality with a spot of fun and forgiveness.

She does not approve of clerics who rock the boat of traditional faith, such as David Jenkins, the former Bishop of Durham, and found John Habgood, the former Archbishop of York, rather too cerebral for her taste. The fact that he has the same, extremely limited, capacity for small talk as herself meant that there were often terrible longueurs when they met.

None of the clerics who had been close to her knows when she prays, though they feel quite sure that she does. One who has noticed that she likes to put on a headscarf and walk her dogs in the Park at Windsor suspects that that is where she does a lot of her praying. In the last fifty years, she has certainly had a great deal to pray about.

'Mummy must not be denied anything'

5 The Indulgent Daughter

From the very beginning of her reign, the Queen had problems with her family. It could hardly have been otherwise. After all, her accession to the throne meant that, of necessity, her mother was dethroned. Suddenly, the woman who had breathed new life into a faltering monarchy after the Abdication was no longer a principal player. She had become, on the face of things, a back number.

The palaces whose social life she had fashioned so brilliantly for fifteen years were no longer hers to command. The courtiers who had hastened to fulfil her every whim now looked elsewhere for their orders. The spotlight in which, like any accomplished actress, she had revelled now shed its light elsewhere, leaving her in the dark and in the wings. She had been stripped of almost everything that mattered to her: husband, position, homes.

Even her access to the royal coffers depended on the generosity of her daughter. As one long-serving courtier put it bluntly, 'She was no longer the boss'; and she did not like it one little bit. 'She was a Leo,' said a member of her family, 'and, like all Leos, she didn't enjoy being number two.' Little wonder that even this most ebullient and optimistic of women could write, in a letter to the poet Edith Sitwell, that she was 'engulfed by great black clouds of unhappiness and misery'.

The new young Queen was fully aware of the depth of her mother's anguish and despair. Standing with her private secretary, Martin Charteris, in her office at Clarence House, where she was still living only three weeks after coming to the throne, she saw her mother driving up in a car and remarked anxiously: 'Here comes the problem!' She was not exaggerating. Quite naturally, she felt guilty that, unable to resist the relentless laws of the succession, she was herself the unwitting agent of her mother's demotion. Both the royal coffers and the monarchy's ability to adjust to a radically different age were to pay heavily to assuage that guilt over the next half-century.

The first thing the Queen had to do was find a house where her mother would be happy to live. The Queen Mother did not want to move from Buckingham Palace. If she had had to, her first choice would have been Marlborough House, with its grand staircase, four vast reception rooms and endless bedrooms. It was in need of considerable renovation, but had plenty of garages and stables. That, however, was not an option, because Marlborough House was already occupied by the Dowager Queen Mary, then in her eighty-fifth year; and the Queen felt she could hardly ask her mother to move in with her own mother-in-law. It would have seemed too much like a dumping-ground for retired Queens.

So far as the Queen Mother was concerned, the other option – Clarence House – seemed, as one of her ladies-in-waiting put it, 'a terrific come-down when you've been Queen and lived in very grand houses like Buckingham Palace and Windsor'. In the bleak days after her husband's death, she dismissed it scathingly as 'a horrid little house' even though that was where her daughter and Prince Philip had been living after it had been renovated for them. It might be suitable for the Gloucesters or other high-ranking royal dependants, but *not* for an anointed Queen. It was, she implied, like being pushed out to live in the lodge while your offspring took over the main house. In fact, it is a splendid residence on four storeys next door, so to speak, to St James's Palace. It was built in 1824 for William IV when he was Duke of Clarence.

With the issue still unresolved, she made what many of those close to her, including the Queen, regarded as a melodramatic and irrational gesture – 'a typical example of widowitis', as one who is herself a widow put it. Driving with friends in Caithness, in the far north of Scotland, she spotted a castle which, at that stage, was little better than a ruin and decided to buy it. No matter that the winds off the nearby sea were so strong that a gardener remembered cabbage heads being torn from their stalks and blown over the wall. Here was real solitude to which she could escape with her grief. The Castle of Mey, as she renamed it, would also be a home that belonged to her, unlike any of the other places where she now stayed. Later, she sometimes wondered why she had ever bought it. At the time, according to her niece, Lady Mary Clayton, she even thought of retiring there.

She might have continued to be both sunk in despair and a considerable anxiety to the Queen. Then came a decisive and unexpected intervention by the Prime Minister, Winston Churchill. 'In August of the year in which the King died,' said one of the Queen Mother's ladies-in-waiting who had been told the story by one of her predecessors in the job, 'at a time when the Queen Mother was seriously considering retiring from public life, Churchill was staying at Balmoral. He went over to see her at Birkhall, a house on the Balmoral estate to which she had moved when Elizabeth became Queen and, not to mince words, gave her a considerable talking-to.

'He impressed upon her that she could not be like Queen Victoria and shrink away from public life, that she must make the break and come back into the world, because she still had a role to play. In particular, he made the point that her daughter, the new Queen, to whom he had obviously spoken about it, was very young and would need all her support. I think that turned it for her.'

Even so, as the Queen soon discovered, her mother was still not reconciled to the demeaning prospect of replacing her at Clarence House. When Queen Mary died in the spring of 1953 and Marlborough House no longer had a royal tenant, she made it clear that she regarded the problem as solved. She would go there, even though – according to Lady Mary Clayton – she thought it had only one bathroom.

The trouble was that the royal coffers were simply not up to it. 'When they examined the state of the finances,' recalled Sir Edward Ford, 'they decided that the money probably wouldn't run to Marlborough House. If the Queen Mother had attempted to live on Queen Mary's scale, who had a staff of eighty at one time, it couldn't have been managed with costs rising as they were.'

It was not easy, however, to convince the Queen Mother that Marlborough House was simply not on. As Ford says, 'She never had any idea of economic living.' Her secretary, Sir Arthur Penn, had to struggle very hard to persuade her

to give up the idea. 'They had an endless correspondence about it,' says one of her aides. Penn pointed out that it would be far too large and expensive, given that she would no longer be taking any part in investitures or receiving new ambassadors. Since there appeared to be no alternative, she eventually gave way. Her cars, at least for the time being, could be kept at Buckingham Palace.

The Queen did her best to sugar the pill by letting it be known that Mummy must not be denied anything else. No doubt aware of this decree, Penn always insisted that the Queen Mother must be given whatever she wanted. The result was that, over the next six years, very large sums of money from the royal coffers were spent not only on rebuilding the Castle of Mey and completely refurbishing Clarence House but also on giving Birkhall a major facelift with a splendid new drawing-room and half a dozen extra bedrooms. As if all that were not enough, the Queen Mother still had Royal Lodge, the country house in the middle of Windsor Great Park, which King George V had given her and her husband in 1931 when they were Duke and Duchess of York.

'The Queen always insisted that Mummy shouldn't be troubled in the way she wanted to live,' said one of the Queen Mother's close friends. 'She felt very fiercely that it was terrible that she should have been widowed at the age of fifty-one.' It was a piece of kindly indulgence which was, perhaps, appropriate for a widowed mother, but the fact that it went on for half a century, that the Queen Mother was treated like a delicate meringue who might fall to pieces if her lifestyle was curtailed in any way, proved very expensive indeed. It did also, in the view of courtiers who both loved and admired the Queen Mother, make her 'frightfully spoilt', as one put it. The Queen's indulgence towards her mother, moreover, was to be repeated in her dealings with her children.

In 1976, she bought Gatcombe Park in Gloucestershire with 733 acres for Princess Anne and Mark Phillips at a price (then very substantial indeed) of between £500,000 and £750,000. In 1989, she financed the building of Sunninghill Park, a sprawling ranch-like mansion in Ascot, for her third child Prince Andrew and his wife, the former Sarah Ferguson: cost, £3.5 million. In 1997, she leased Bagshot Park, a vast, 57-room mansion on 88 acres for a mere £50,000 a year to her youngest child, Prince Edward and his wife Sophie, when estate agents reckoned that the £15-million house would have fetched ten times as much on the open market for its owners, the Crown Estates. The Crown Estates, which

Elizabeth and her mother in 1940.

own a vast collection of land and urban housing mainly in central London, not to mention half of the United Kingdom's entire foreshore, remains the property of the sovereign in right of the Crown and does not belong to the government, though the Queen hands over to the Exchequer any surplus income from its lands.

Senior clerics who have been close to the Queen for many years positively sizzle with disapproval. 'The Queen is tight in her own financial affairs,' said one, 'but she has been very extravagant with her children, she has indulged them terribly financially. She allowed Andrew and Sarah to build that house in Ascot when there were already perfectly good houses available. Sarah couldn't have cared less about the budget, but the Queen didn't come down on her, she just paid up and that was very wrong. There was no possible excuse for it.

'And she bought Gatcombe Park for Anne when, again, there were perfectly good houses empty which Anne could have had. If she'd married Mark Phillips during the war, she'd never have got Gatcombe Park. When it comes to over-indulgence of that kind, the Queen is guilty in spades.'

Perhaps she was trying to compensate for spending so little time with all her children. When Mabel Anderson, a nanny who had brought up Edward, moved in to look after Anne's children, she asked the Queen bluntly, 'Who is going to look after Edward now, because you won't!' The Queen protested that Mabel had no right to say such things. Yet Edward was the child who, according to one of her longest-serving ladies-in-waiting, the Queen was supposed to regard as 'her ewe-lamb'. The same lady, however, said that Prince Andrew had always been the Queen's favourite. 'He's really a Prince Philip without Prince Philip's intellect,' she explained, 'a real macho type and that appeals to her!'

Yet her extravagance with her children was mere chicken-feed when compared to the limitless benevolence which the Queen displayed towards her mother for half a century. Rightly assuming that she had a financial free rein, the Queen Mother soon showed the rest of the royal field a clean pair of heels in the high-spending stakes. 'If there had been two of them who spent money as she does,' Lord Carnarvon told me a few years ago, 'there'd be nothing left in the coffers now. She buys new outfits like you buy brown eggs!'

The Queen occasionally made feeble efforts to rein back her mother's profligacy, but always failed miserably. 'She did once affectionately suggest that her mother should not buy quite so much new bloodstock in one particular year,' recalled one of the Queen Mother's friends, 'but nonetheless a huge bill arrived in due course. All the Queen felt she could do was send her mother a note which simply said, "Oh dear, Mummy!"'

Every year, the Queen had to subsidize her mother massively, since the Queen Mother's annual Civil List allowance – £643,000 at the time of her death – did little more than cover the cost of her numerous staff. 'The Queen Mother's Civil List payment was just the tip of the iceberg really,' said a former senior adviser with a detailed knowledge of the royal finances. 'In my time, there was private money, managed by Morgan Grenfell, which the Queen Mother regarded as the late King's money, though in fact it was the Queen's – and that was used to top her up. The top-up was huge. It often went into seven figures a year. She was a very expensive lady.'

Courtiers who themselves were on very modest salaries were astonished at the extravagance of the Queen Mother's spending. 'She had none of the usual Scottish carefulness,' said Edward Ford. 'She didn't seem to know anything about money.' Her own staff were equally astounded. 'She had absolutely not a clue about money,' one of her ladies-in-waiting told me. Others simply admired the fact that that was not any part of her mind-set. 'She simply didn't think about it,' said another lady-in-waiting, 'and why should she?' She affected not even to be able to remember the name of Buckingham Palace's former finance director, Sir Michael Peat.

She lived in almost Edwardian splendour. 'She had a very grand life,' said a St James's Palace insider who knew Clarence House well. 'She had five or six cars with a special series of number plates, three chauffeurs and five chefs at her various houses – and that was just the start of it. Clarence House was another world, a time-warp. Whenever I went there, three liveried footmen brought in a really full tea. In my view, it was exactly what it should be like, providing it was not public money that was being spent.' In the Queen Mother's mind, she was simply maintaining what she considered to be the style of an anointed monarch. Tellingly, she still – like the Queen – signed herself 'Elizabeth R' until the day she died.

When it was reported three years ago that she was running a £4 million overdraft at Coutts and that she had a staff of fifty, the only surprise among those who knew her was that the figure had been set so disappointingly low. The Prince of Wales, far from chiding his grandmother for her extravagance, merely smiled wryly and remarked that if the reported shortfall were only a tenth of the real figure, the media were at least aiming in the right direction. Martin Charteris, too, thought the figure 'far too low', while one of the Queen Mother's friends remarked with a grin, 'I would have thought you could add another nought to that!'

As for the size of the Queen Mother's staff, she may once have thought that Clarence House was 'a horrid little house', but she certainly did not have a horrid little staff. If anything, the reported figure of fifty was probably slightly understated. According to those who knew the place well, there was a staff of between thirty and forty at Clarence House alone – 'Two pages, four footmen, two ladies' maids, three chauffeurs, two chefs with four helpers, a housekeeper and five housemaids, three lady secretaries, three orderlies, several gardeners plus the Queen Mother's secretary and treasurer, not to mention equerries.' Lunch guests observed that there were always three or four waiting at table. At Royal Lodge in Windsor Great Park, where she spent weekends when she was staying in London, there were ten more servants, and yet more at both Birkhall and Mey.

The Queen Mother certainly used her daughter's generosity to good effect. She was a superb hostess, the party girl to end all party girls and a general life-enhancer, to the benefit of everyone who knew or served her. 'I knew her for at least thirty years,' said Lord Norwich, 'and she had a simply marvellous capacity for enjoyment. You always felt she was having a wonderful time, because she was either rocking with laughter at your stories or telling frightfully good ones herself. It was infectious. She enjoyed herself so much that everyone else felt the same.'

Her parties seemed to be never-ending. There were racing parties, fishing parties, stalking parties for Prince Charles's friends, parties for the young, parties for fellow geriatrics. 'She had parties every single week for the whole of September,' said one of her nieces who is also a lady-in-waiting. 'Each one of them went on from Monday until Saturday, and then a new crowd showed up on the following Monday.'

By the end of the autumn party round, her ladies-in-waiting were always out on their feet. 'I just couldn't do those parties of hers,' complained one who is now in her eighties. 'They were so unflagging! That's the reason I once tried to resign, but she just said "Congratulations! Life becomes such fun after you're eighty!" One slept for twenty-four, even forty-eight, hours after a month of it. It was totally exhausting.'

Not for the Queen Mother. 'I remember going to Birkhall a couple of years ago,' said a fifty-year-old friend of Prince Charles, 'and, at midnight, there was a group of so-called young men sitting round the dinner table. We'd been stalking and shooting on the hill all day, and she herself had been outside for much of it. But whereas most of us had our eyes half-closed, she was still the life and soul of the party. One had to remind oneself that she was ninety-seven.'

Nor did age wither her taste for gin. One long-standing friend remembers being in charge of the drinks at a lunch party given for the Queen Mother. 'I knew she liked a big gin and Dubonnet,' he recalled, 'so I gave her a whopper, which I suppose amounted to a triple, and then went round the other people. When I came back to her, four or five minutes later, her glass was already empty, so I offered her the same again. "So delicious," she said. "Perhaps just a little more." She had three of those triples before lunch and her fair share of wine during it. Yet, afterwards, she walked briskly for several hundred yards in a dead straight line, talking lucidly the whole time. She was the greatest living advertisement for gin.'

Each year, on her birthday, Ivor Spencer of the Guild of International Professional Toastmasters presented the Queen Mother with a nebuchadnezzar of champagne – the equivalent of twenty bottles. 'It'll be very nice when your family come,' Spencer said to her at a recent celebration. 'Even if they don't,' replied the Queen Mother, 'I'll polish it off myself!'

Even when she was bent on solitude, which was rarely, the Queen Mother was unfailingly courteous to people who would normally be regarded as intruders. 'She had a little two-roomed shack on Invercauld, the next estate to Balmoral,' said one of her nieces, 'and we sometimes went up there for a break. It's a terrible drive, the road is pretty rough, but it's very peaceful and the views are wonderful.

'Five years ago, we made the trek and, to my horror, saw a man and woman – obviously hikers – sitting on the grass in front of the hut. "Oh, what a bore," I thought. "How can we get rid of them?" That wasn't the Queen Mother's reaction at all. She got out, chatted them up, gave them a couple of gin and tonics and sent them on their way, glowing. Nobody else in her family would have done that.'

It is easy to see from all this why the Queen has had to bail her mother out so substantially over the years. The fact that the Queen did not feel able to curtail her mother's spending, moreover, has done little for the monarchy's image among its more parsimonious critics.

When the overdraft story broke, courtiers who had been earnestly trying to sell the idea that it had become a frugal, value-for-money operation were thrown into a flat spin. Thinking the Queen Mother invulnerable, their strategy had been to observe a vow of silence about her spending. Now they had to massage reported 'facts' as best they could. 'We told the media that her staff was only half the fifty which had been reported,' confessed a Buckingham Palace insider at the time, 'but the truth was that we hadn't a clue as to the precise number. The Queen Mother kept these things very much to herself – she was a complete autocrat.

'There was also a real feeling of helplessness in the Palace that there was nothing we could do about it, because the Queen Mother was out of control and there was no real will to control her. It certainly didn't help in trying to present an image of a more transparent, value-for-money operation if it seemed that there was a bottomless pit of cash.

'There was also resentment in some quarters here that, while *we* were not very well paid, there was all this money sloshing around. People felt a sense of selfishness on the Queen Mother's part, that she was getting as much as possible from the public purse and, in some ways, had spent her life living on it. People asked the question, "What is she putting back into the country? And where is the hospital endowed in her name?" But the Queen was very much her parents' daughter and she wouldn't interfere at all with her mother's attitudes.'

Nor did the Queen's indulgence of her mother's high-spending habits affect only the monarchy's image, because the Queen Mother's extravagant lifestyle has been taken up with enthusiasm by her eldest grandson, Prince Charles. If your mother never tells you that you are wonderful and Granny always does, whom are you going to imitate? It is the Queen Mother, not the Queen or Prince Philip, whom Charles has taken as his model, with all that that implies for the future of the monarchy.

Her influence on him has been immense. Members of her own family say that he is the son she never had. Clerics who know Prince Charles intimately believe that, given his cool and distant relationship with the Queen, Granny was the mother he felt he never had. She was the only member of the Royal Family to whom he could talk about his personal problems.

'The result,' said a former senior courtier, 'is that his attitudes are very much like hers. He mirrors her view of life and the monarchy. His mantras are the same as hers: he makes exactly the same noises about the decline of standards, that things are not what they used to be and so on. He is his grandmother's voice. In family gatherings, they always stood very much together.'

Charles, inspired by his grandmother's limpet-like attachment to the splendours of tradition, seems bent on proving that things *can* be just what they used to be. 'The Prince of Wales tries to emulate Granny in the grand life he leads,' said one of those who knows him well. 'His parents and other members of the Royal Family think he is far too grand, but his grandmother encouraged him to be like that, to indulge himself, to be really royal in the old style.'

He has certainly followed her lead. Like her, he has a fleet of cars, including two Aston Martins, a Bentley, a leased £160,000 Vantage and two estate cars, all for his own private use. Like her, he has a small regiment of servants – three butlers, four valets, three chauffeurs, four chefs and ten gardeners. His annual arts weekend at Sandringham in March, according to one of those involved in the planning, must cost at least £20,000.

Those who have been guests at these weekends can quite see why. To them, he seems to be trying to out-granny Granny. 'To start with,' said a man who is not easily impressed by displays of wealth, 'there must have been twenty or thirty servants when I went. Everybody was given their own individual valet or maid and each evening, as we came down to dinner, our jaws dropped open at the splendour of the table, the silver, the decorations, the flowers, the statues and the lighting. It was different on each of the three nights – an unbelievable display, absolutely dazzling.

'Charles has got the same incredible instinct for style as the Queen Mother had, but she never went over the top. He does. He knows that the Queen and Prince Philip would be horrified if they saw it, but that Granny would have loved it.' Although she was deeply fond of her mother, the Queen often felt thoroughly irritated at the Queen Mother's indulgence of Charles's foibles and resented the fact that she too often gave him a soft ride when a gentle word of reproof might have helped him more.

Not only did Prince Charles adore his grandmother, he was also constantly in touch with her, though not with his mother. 'He was absolutely besotted with her,' said a senior member of his staff. 'He doted on her from an early age and did so right to the end. If only the Queen were like her, and he felt he could just pick up a phone and chat as he did all the time with the Queen Mother.' According to Lord Hurd, the Queen has made something of a point of refusing to talk to her children on the telephone.

'Whether he was at St James's, Highgrove or with friends in the country,' the aide went on, 'if the call came through from Granny, he'd take it, even if he was in a room full of people. He'll never do that with other members of

the Royal Family. If it was her, he'd just go off into a corner with the mobile and have a giggle.

'If he was here at St James's and she was in residence at Clarence House, he was constantly popping across the yard to see her. If he didn't go in the morning, he'd have a drink with her before supper. Princess Anne lives just next door to us here, but he never does that with her.'

While Charles sometimes seems uneasy with his mother, everyone noticed how radiantly happy he was with his grandmother. 'It was so lovely to see them together,' said one of the Queen Mother's ladies-in-waiting. 'He'd arrive at a picnic at Balmoral and say to her, "Oh, Your Majesty, I'm graciously honoured to see you!" and she'd reply, "Would it please Your Royal Highness to have a drink?" Then he'd kiss her all the way up her arms. If the Queen Mother had asked him to swim the Channel, he would have done it.' For a small lady, she cast a very long shadow over the style which the monarchy may well try to adopt if and when Charles becomes King.

The Queen Mother also had a great deal to say about the way in which the monarchy was conducted over the past half-century, and she did not hesitate to say it. She had enormous if hidden influence on the Queen and, since she wanted to change nothing but her outfits, was always fiercely opposed to reform of any kind, however minor. 'Her mind-set,' according to one of the Queen's former private secretaries, 'was pre-war,' and many of the principal courtiers of the last four decades are convinced that the monarchy would have modernized itself far more rapidly had she not remained a force to be reckoned with.

Over those years, courtiers at Buckingham Palace learnt that, if they wanted anything changed, they first had to make sure that the Queen herself was so convinced of the idea that she would not allow her mother to veto it. No matter what the topic under discussion – all the way from the Queen's decision to pay tax to the exact form of the Court Circular – the Queen Mother's view always had to be taken into account.

The Queen Mother outside Clarence House on her eightieth birthday, 4 August 1980.

'From time to time,' said a former senior courtier, 'I'd hear my colleagues remark, "The Queen is going to have to sell this to her mother." There'd be issues where the Queen would say in a dead voice, "I'd better ask Mummy about that," knowing that the Queen Mother was going to have a very decided view and, second, that it would be negative. Everyone in the Palace realized that, in family matters, the Queen Mother was not to be crossed. She had a huge influence on her daughter, though not necessarily the last word.

'The truth is that having her mother around all the time was an enormous burden on the Queen because she was not entirely free to be her own person. She was always aware of the shadow of her mother, a strong granny who ruled the roost. I once sat next to the Queen Mother at Sandringham after the Queen had allowed a photographer into the house to take a few shots after a reception and before lunch. The Queen Mother railed on and on about it. "Why does the Queen let these people into the house?" she said. "I'd never allow them into my home!" So there was pressure on the Queen even on small things – and even in her own home!

'The Royal Family all deferred to the Queen Mother. When she spoke, everyone listened. The Queen is such a giving person and had such a deep well of affection for her mother that she would sometimes remain silent. She would certainly do anything to avoid having to tell her mother to get back into her box.

'You have to remember that the Queen is both very dutiful and very much the daughter of her parents. "I'm not going to do that," she will say, "because the King never did." So she is already conservative by nature, but the influence of the Queen Mother only served to strengthen that conservatism. She may have rolled her eyes about Mummy, but she still preferred to go along with her.'

'I have seen the Royal Family together three or four times,' said a bishop who has preached at Sandringham, 'and the Queen Mother was, you might say, the atmosphere of the Windsors. When she came into the room, there was a new feeling among them, a feeling of reverence. She was so small in her later years you could almost step over her, but she had enormous background influence.' According to her own aides, Princess Diana had world-class manipulative skills, but even she was a mere novice when compared to the Queen Mother.

Courtiers whose task it has been to try to drag the monarchy into the modern age found her a most formidable opponent, a perilous rock around whom they had to navigate. 'The Queen's relationship to her mother was more complex than you might think,' said one of the leading reformers, 'and I was always very careful to steer clear of Clarence House, because I knew that what I wanted to do would be looked on unfavourably in that quarter. So far as the Queen Mother was concerned, I was the devil incarnate.

'She was totally opposed to Buckingham Palace being opened – there was a frightful row about that – and equally against the disappearance of the Queen's Flight, the end of the Royal Yacht and the "dumbing-down" of the Royal Train to allow it to be used by ministers, not to mention the Queen agreeing to pay tax. It was my job to see that she didn't influence the Queen. Feathers did fly, but I kept my head down. Her presence just complicated everything.'

It was apparent to all those who were involved in the process of reform that the Queen simply lacked either the willingness or the ability to take on her mother face to face. So, for example, when arrangements had to be made to bring back the Duchess of Windsor's body from Paris for burial at Frogmore, she sent one of her senior aides to tell her mother about them. 'It was "Let someone else catch it in the neck,"' said a former courtier, 'and that applied to any awkward question. She simply did not want to have that kind of discussion with her mother.' Some of those who went in her stead felt that they would have preferred to go armour-clad.

Over the years, the Queen Mother often lost the battle, but the affair of the Ascot Office, insignificant in itself, illustrates the extraordinary power which she could generate. At the beginning of the 1990s, after Buckingham Palace had appointed Michael Peat as finance director to give the royal accounts a thorough overhaul, he mooted the idea of moving the Ascot Office out of St James's Palace as one of a series of cost-cutting measures.

As courtiers and former courtiers tell it, the Ascot Office is a small operation whose modest task is to keep a register of members for the Royal Enclosure and send out the appropriate entry vouchers. It is not, as Peat immediately noticed, part of the Queen's household and operates at full throttle for only a few months of the year.

Since Ascot itself was, by that time, a fully self-funding commercial operation, he could see no obvious reason why the Office should be taking up several hundred square feet of valuable Palace space, always a commodity in short supply. Scenting useful savings, he asked the then Keeper of the Privy Purse, Major Sir Shane Blewitt, to write a paper setting out the benefits of moving the Ascot Office out of St James's.

It sounded an unimpeachable idea, but Peat had reckoned without the Queen Mother and her influence. She somehow found out what was afoot. This was scarcely surprising, since she spoke to the Queen on the telephone

every day and, in any case, the man then running the Ascot Office, Sir Piers Bengough, was one of her oldest racing friends. Whoever told her, she did not like the idea one little bit. The Office had been at St James's for years. Why on earth *should* it be forced to move out?

When they heard that the Queen Mother had entered the lists, some of the men of reform quailed. 'I said immediately that it was a no-win situation,' recalled one senior courtier. 'I could see that the place was right on the Queen Mother's doorstep, not twenty yards from Clarence House, and knew that the Queen would never allow her to be disturbed in her own world. I decided that it wasn't worth the fight, that in this case discretion was the better part of valour.'

Just how wise he had been soon became clear, when a less prudent axeman put the scheme to the Queen late one Thursday night just after she had arrived back from a State visit. He asked whether she could spare him a few minutes before she went down to Windsor on the following day, knowing perfectly well that she would be ambushed by the Queen Mother once she arrived there and went over to Royal Lodge for a drink.

At first, everything went smoothly. The Queen nodded when he explained the plan and seemed perfectly happy with the proposal. But when he saw her again on the following Tuesday, she seemed a totally different woman. Indeed, it was the only time in all the courtier's years of service that he had ever seen her lose her cool. She was, or so it appeared to him, extremely cross and totally unreasonable.

His reading of the situation was that the Queen had been 'boxed in by Mummy', caught in a very unpleasant crossfire, landed with a row she did not want. He could see no point in prolonging the discussion, so he simply let the Queen rant on for four or five minutes and then retired hurt. His conclusion was quite simple: when Mummy dug her toes in, that was it. The moving of the Ascot Office was never discussed again. 'On issues of that kind,' sighed another Palace insider, 'you took on the Queen Mother at your peril!'

'The Queen,' said one of her former assistant private secretaries, 'would be very happy to get rid of the Ascot Office, but there are certain things one didn't do while Mummy was still alive.' So the Office is still at St James's, courtesy of the Queen Mother.

The Queen Mother's funeral service, Westminster Abbey, 9 April 2002.

The Queen, of course, never allowed her mother's influence to extend into her constitutional role as head of State. 'That,' she would say to courtiers when such issues arose, 'has nothing to do with Mummy.' Even so, it seems quite extraordinary that, in almost every other way, she allowed herself to be in hock to her mother, and for so long. In her defence, it could be said that she has a relentlessly demanding job which constantly exposes her to the public gaze, and that the last thing she needs – if she wants to keep her eye on the ball – is emotionally exhausting stand-offs with members of her family.

Given the fact that her mother was around all the time – 'She's eternal,' as Prince Philip once wryly remarked – appeasement may well have seemed the only practical policy unless she wanted to risk a full-scale and long-running family feud. That, nonetheless, is still a rather thin defence. Appeasement is apt to produce dictators and is never particularly good for either side.

On the other hand, the accommodation which the Queen made with a determined and controlling mother says a great deal for both her grace and her modesty. 'One Sunday when I was in waiting at Sandringham,' recalled one of the Queen Mother's aides, 'I was walking behind her after church, relieving her of the flowers presented to her by members of the public because it was close to her birthday. The Queen was doing exactly the same thing, acting in effect as a second lady-in-waiting. "Oh darling," she said to her mother, "why don't you go to that side? They don't want to see me, they want to see you."' It was the same at dinner parties in Windsor, according to the former Dean, Michael Mann. 'The Queen,' he says, 'would always stand back and push her mother forward.'

Again and again, she would leave the stage free for her partly because she knew that the Queen Mother was far more adept at chatting people up. 'When they came out of the chapel at Royal Lodge together,' said one of the Queen's former secretaries, 'they would walk past the rest of the congregation on their way back to the house. Sometimes, that'd include a whole crowd of law students from a residential course at Cumberland Lodge – a large building in Windsor Great Park which the Queen allows to be used for such things – and, whereas the Queen Mother would spend twenty minutes or so talking to them, the Queen would walk quite fast along the line and then stand waiting at the end.'

Sometimes, she could only marvel at the magic touch with people which her mother possessed in abundance and she, sadly, lacks. 'Two young men from a course at Cumberland Lodge came to Matins one Sunday,' recalled a former chaplain. 'I could see immediately that they'd been having far too much to drink and were distinctly the worse for wear. I'm not sure why they'd come.

They didn't join in the service and couldn't wait to get away at the end. But, as they tried to shuffle off, the Queen Mother spotted them and said, "Hello!"

'They just mumbled a reply, looking thoroughly grey. At that point, I felt I should step in, so I said, "Ma'am, they were at a rather good party last night." "Was it a very good party?" she asked, those blue eyes of hers twinkling. "Very good," one of them muttered. "Well then," she said with a gentle smile, "I think I ought to leave you alone," and floated quietly away. She was ninety-three at the time.'

The Queen recognized that that kind of humorous finesse is usually beyond her. On the other hand, she often watched her mother's infinitely more expansive style with an amused and slightly sardonic tolerance. 'She adores her mother,' the late Lord Charteris once told me, 'but somewhat disapproves of her when she thinks she is being too fulsome, laying on the Gaiety Girl act a bit thick. She regards it as rather dishonest. The Queen is far more honest than her mother, die-straight, but she knows there is no point in competing. She's bad at opening up partly because her mother is so good at it.'

The atmosphere of the two Queens' London homes reflected both the difference in their styles and the fact that the Queen Mother had far greater freedom than her daughter. Buckingham Palace is, perforce, taut and business-like; Clarence House was markedly merrier.

'Our place,' said one of the Queen Mother's ladies-in-waiting, 'was altogether jollier. We liked each other much better than the people over the road, and that came straight down from her. We looked at what goes on in Buckingham Palace with amazement and a degree of smugness. One reason it wasn't like that at Clarence House was that none of us either had a career to build or, at our age, was trying to build one!'

In public and in private, however, the meticulous deference the two women showed each other was a model of courtesy. 'When I went to preach at Sandringham,' recalled an Anglican bishop, 'I was standing next to the Queen Mother before she went up to bed on Sunday night and she said, "It's been lovely having you, do come again." Then she turned to the Queen and immediately apologized. "Oh, how rude of me, darling," she said. "It isn't for me to invite anyone to Sandringham." She was extremely deferential to the sovereignty of her daughter.'

It cannot have been easy for the Queen to have her mother there or thereabouts all the time, however much she loved her. She is also quite aware that it must have been a hundred times more difficult for Prince Philip; and she had to take account of the fact that neither her mother nor her sister, Princess Margaret, liked Philip at all in the early years.

For one thing, Philip – at the outset – had an irresistible desire to change all the things that he thought needed changing about the way in which the royal palaces were run. But to his intense frustration, this natural chief executive, who instinctively wants to run everything in which he is involved, soon found that he was part of a court determined to stop him changing anything that mattered, and that his chief opponent was that arch-conservative, his mother-in-law. 'I think Prince Philip found it incredibly difficult to make any changes,' said one of the Queen Mother's ladies-in-waiting, 'and that was largely my boss's fault. If he wanted to change the staff at Balmoral, for example, she would just say "No!" and that was it.'

Philip's position when Elizabeth came to the throne was unenviable to say the least. A naval career was no longer open to him. He could not live where he wanted. He was told in 1952 that, by order of Winston Churchill, his children could not bear his adopted name of Mountbatten. His very income came from his wife. All of which conspired to make him feel less than a man and certainly less than a prince. As if that were not enough, he was surrounded by courtiers who regarded him as an upstart foreign parasite who had to be put firmly in the place they thought appropriate.

'He was very badly treated by the Queen's then private secretaries, Alan Lascelles and Michael Adeane,' said one of their successors in that office. 'When he arrived, they determined that he wasn't going to play any part on their side of the house. They'd dealt with the King and had no intention of letting anyone but the Queen see the red boxes or give advice about their content. They decided to shut Philip out completely, and they succeeded.' They need not have bothered. Philip never intended to run the Queen from the back seat in constitutional matters.

'The old Establishment,' recalled a senior courtier at Windsor, 'were also privately and publicly contemptuous of his background. "Is he Greek? Is he Danish? Is he German?" they would sniff. They also didn't care for his link with his uncle Lord Mountbatten, whom many senior courtiers regard as a tiresome, pushy, egocentric man and who, in many ways, was Philip's greatest embarrassment. So all the time in those early years, he was faced with a series of slights, intended and unintended, from people who had written him off as a greedy parvenu.

'Philip once told me that, when he put up the idea of the Duke of Edinburgh's Award Scheme, the then Education Secretary, Sir David Eccles, said to him, "I hear you're trying to invent something like the Hitler Youth!" The insult to a man who had risked his life for Britain during the war was unforgivable and unforgettable.'

Philip was conscious, too, that, although he had spent most of his childhood in Britain and was, indeed, related to the Royal Family, he was still not a fully paid-up member of that world – not Eton and the Guards, and quite obviously not an English country gentleman with an appropriately laid-back style.

The man-in-the-street might think of him as a typical English aristocrat, but English aristocrats had other ideas. Those who did not like him, and they were many, simply wrote him off as 'a bit of a Kraut'. Even those who were fond of him, such as one of the Queen's longest-serving aides, regarded him as 'very Germanic, very hard-working, very tidy-minded, incredibly knowledgeable and clever' – a description that makes even his virtues sound rather alarming.

So, at Court, and in his own social circle, he was – and is still – regarded as a somewhat alien figure. 'One of my predecessors, who was Eton and the Guards,' said a former courtier, 'always told me that I should remember that Philip is quite foreign. And he really is something of a chameleon. He's had, to some extent, to take on the colour, trappings and attitudes of the British, and he's not quite made it. When you do that, there's bound to be a bogusness somewhere, and it's not his fault. He's assumed an unreal identity and that must affect you.

'When you're talking to him and he's at his nicest, he's as English as they come, and yet he isn't quite. One small thing is his suits. If you've been part of the crowd who've been through Eton and the Guards, there's a certain kind of suit you're expected to wear. It's a pinstripe with a white line. I know only two people who wear pinstriped suits with a blue or red line and one of them is Prince Philip.

'Another thing is that you'd put your handkerchief in your top pocket so that it hangs down in a slightly foppish way, whereas his is always in a straight line. His argument for wearing it like that would be quite simple: "It's there to blow your nose on, not for decoration!"'

'He has had to try to learn the English upper-class way,' said an Anglican bishop who greatly admires him, 'and he's not done it very well. He had a mother who didn't know where her roots were, and there is in him both a rootlessness and a confused sense of identity. He's never known quite where he stands, partly because he's always been treated by the Establishment as an outsider who had to be put up with. That has given him a strong feeling of Philip *contra mundum*. It is hardly surprising that he sometimes seems like a lonely fellow.'

Philip had few, if any, male confidants with whom he felt he could discuss absolutely anything and was faced by a strongly entrenched female triumvirate without whom nothing could be changed. He nevertheless had no intention of being put down. His behaviour could scarcely have been more different from the bland, play-it-safe-at-all-costs style typical of so many European monarchies over the past half-century. He always said precisely what he thought, often with scant regard for the consequences. The blue touch-paper was always alight and, as a result, he has always had an endless capacity for causing either amusement or offence.

Senior Buckingham Palace insiders felt the lash of his tongue with painful regularity. At a meeting in the library in the 1970s, he famously told Major Sir Rennie Maudslay, then keeper of the Privy Purse: 'You're just a silly little Whitehall twit. You don't trust me and I don't trust you!' before sending a two-page letter of apology, saying that he didn't know what had got into him. Whatever it was, it got into him fairly often.

When Chief Anyaoku, then Secretary-General of the Commonwealth, arrived at the Palace in full Nigerian dress, Philip laughed and said, 'You look as if you're ready for bed.' And when a farmer's wife from Northern Ireland flew to London for a charity event in Chelsea, she was amazed when Philip said to the Ulsterwoman next in line: 'So, you managed to get here without having your knickers blown off!'

So here was another powerful character, with volcanic energy and views diametrically opposed to those of the Queen Mother whom the Queen had to take account of. She had somehow to make sure he found a new and satisfying role so that some, at least, of his profound frustrations could be diverted into fruitful activity. Any woman who has had to reconcile a strong-minded husband and an equally strong-minded mother while trying to give proper attention to a very demanding job can readily understand the dilemmas with which the Queen was confronted. She could – and did – give him the royal estates to run, and hand over to him the task of bringing up their children, but, in large part, he had to fashion a new role for himself.

The Queen also had to find a way of dealing with his explosive nature, the fact that – because of his frustrations – he was apt to loose off a broadside at any moment. Perhaps she was helped by the fact that she had watched her mother coping with the King's frequent 'gnashes'. 'I've seen her driven almost to drink by Philip's behaviour,' Lord Charteris told me. ' "I'm simply not going to appear until Philip is in a better temper," she would say.'

'He could be very rough on her,' agreed another former senior courtier. 'I've heard him say to her, "You're talking rubbish," scores of times. He even called her "a bloody fool" over breakfast. Yet I never heard her snap back. Sometimes her technique when Philip was rude was to put up a smokescreen. She'd change the subject and start talking in riddles. Then he'd be diverted, trying to find out what the hell she was talking about. His mind runs on lines of intellect and so, when she starts saying things that are non-sequiturs, he's lost. It's a bit like the way in which our aircraft used to scatter pieces of aluminium foil during the war to confuse the enemy's radar.'

The Queen had to depend on her own ingenuity because there were precious few other people prepared to stand up to Philip for her. On one rare occasion, a courageous courtier did so. 'There is an old ice cave at Windsor,' he recalled. 'It's in the block behind the castle. On top of the cave is a glass cupola. Some years ago, that glass was broken and became dangerous, so the Department of the Environment submitted a plan to re-do it.

'At lunch one day, Philip – who'd found out that something was going on – attacked her about it. "What's all this, there's nothing wrong with the thing" – that sort of stuff. She didn't try to defend herself. She just said, "I see it when I'm out riding, it's easier to spot from the top of a horse." He sounded off again – "You don't know anything" – until I could bear it no longer. So I said, "*I* do, sir, and the Queen is absolutely right!" He then shut up. He's darn lucky that he can give her a hard time without ever having it held against him.' That is because the Queen loves Philip so much that she is prepared to forgive him almost anything, and because he has been such a stalwart, if sometimes embarrassing, consort.

Throughout their married life, there have been persistent rumours that Philip has had extra-marital affairs, but chapter and verse has been forthcoming for none of them. Of one thing, at least, there is no doubt: his

uninhibited enjoyment of attractive women. 'All the girls in his office,' said one courtier, 'have to be 36–24–36.'

He homes in on pretty girls whenever and wherever they appear. 'There was a reception at the Palace not long ago,' said a former courtier, 'and the wives of staff were lined up to meet members of the Royal Family. My wife looked particularly good, and he went straight for her in a very direct way, closely followed by Prince Andrew. He didn't mince matters. There were three or four other ladies in the line before her, but he was very cursory with them. It was the classic male flirt line, and my wife went puce. He loves having that effect.'

Nor is that at all unusual. 'If an attractive girl comes into the room,' said another former courtier, 'or there's a particularly pretty girl wearing something striking in a line-up, he'll say, "Mm!" very appreciatively, though not in a way that makes you feel embarrassed for the Queen.'

The key question is how far the appreciation goes. I have talked to several of the ladies with whom he is supposed to have had a fling. I have also talked to former courtiers whose candour about the sexual activities of the Royal Family is remarkable.

'If Philip played around, he was bloody clever,' said one who knew him well. 'It certainly wasn't passing women, like Prince Charles. As for him having an affair with Princess Alexandra – never! I was at Cowes with him more than once when the Queen was not there, but I never saw him tiptoeing along the corridors. The people he invited to Cowes Week, like the Westmorlands, always came as couples.

'There were parties at the Royal Yacht squadron, but there were never any nymphets in the background. I never saw any sign of impropriety. I didn't see him snogging on the dance floor, with his hand on somebody's breast or bum, and I was with him on several occasions when it might have happened.

'As for Prince Charles, at times during the 1970s he was incredibly and naively indiscreet. A whole army of girls enjoyed his favours. If his valet had blown the gaff, it would have been sensational. But I never had any concrete evidence of Philip sleeping with anyone.'

Elizabeth and Philip in Nigeria, on their 1956 tour of Africa.

Every courtier I have spoken to says the same thing. Geoff Williams, his former pilot, is typical. 'I have no information that would make two lines in the *Sun*,' he told me. Crucially, to my mind, Lord Charteris did not believe that Philip played around in any serious way. Charteris was no prude, and had his own extremely well-informed intelligence network.

Philip himself despairs at the persistence of prurient rumours about the nature of his sex life. 'When I see the tabloids,' he once grumbled to Lady Mountbatten, 'I think I might as well have done it.'

But what do the ladies with whom Philip is supposed to have had affairs have to say? 'I know something about these supposed romances,' said one woman who has been friendly with Philip for many years, 'because I've been quoted as having had one. He is the most brilliant dancer, even better than Prince Charles. He's got terrific rhythm, he can dance close or apart, he can even do a bit of rock. When you dance with someone who's attractive, you get quite close to them, and Philip certainly gives you a lot of attention. But he has never, over all these years, done anything remotely improper with me, nor has there ever been an improper suggestion.

'He's accused of having had all these affairs but, on the basis of my own experience, I believe him when he tells me that he hasn't. I know of at least one woman who tried extremely hard to seduce him, but even she didn't succeed. Coming away from him, whether you've just been sitting next to him at a meal or dancing with him, you do feel like a million dollars, because he's very good at making you feel marvellous.'

The lady's husband, like so many of the consorts of those to whom Philip takes a shine, sometimes felt like rather less than a million dollars on these occasions. 'I keep a very close eye on my wife,' he said with a grin, but added that he had spent time on *Britannia* when the Queen was not present, and there was no chance of Philip having conducted an affair. Every minute was accounted for.

'He's very flirtatious,' remarked another charming and attractive woman, now in her middle years, with whom Philip is supposed to have had a fling, 'and I've danced and talked to him a great deal, but I don't think he is a great Lothario. In all my times with him, there has been nothing improper, no immoral suggestion, nothing to break the Commandments.' From someone who was entirely candid with me about the vagaries of her own private life, that seems to me fairly conclusive.

Nevertheless, as courtiers note, Philip makes sure that the guest lists at Sandringham and Balmoral always contain at least one woman he finds attractive. 'When it comes to inviting people,' said one of his lady friends, 'it's the wives he wants to see, not the husbands. And they're there time after time. Penny Romsey (the wife of Lord Mountbatten's grandson, Lord Romsey) is the current favourite and has been for several years. The Queen is incredibly tolerant of the beautiful girls he has to stay. She just says, rather resignedly: "Philip likes to have them around."'

There is, moreover, no evidence that he has ever behaved improperly with Lady Romsey, according to those in the Palace who make it their business to check out such things.

How, though, does all this affect Philip's relationship with the Queen? Old courtiers believe that, because of his flirting, 'things were tricky between them in the early days'. And there was certainly a marked *froideur* after Philip discovered that he could not give his adopted surname to Prince Charles.

Those storms are long past. 'I think the Queen is so sure of his affection now that she's able to take a very liberal view of the way he behaves,' said Michael Mann, the former Dean of Windsor, who knows Philip extremely well. 'He is attracted by very good-looking women, but I don't think he's ever fallen in love with anyone else since they married.'

On the other hand, the Queen would surely be less than human if she were not irritated by the attention Philip pays to his attractive lady friends. Nonetheless, 'He and the Queen usually do share a bed,' said a former courtier. 'If there's an early start, or one of them has a cold, Philip will move into the dressing-room, but normally they have this great big double bed. Why not? They're very fond of each other.'

When they were on board *Britannia*, on the other hand, they did have separate bedrooms; and the occasion, in the summer of 1982, when Michael Fagan, who believed that his father was Rudolf Hess, broke into the Queen's bedroom in Buckingham Palace at 7 a.m., was clearly one of the times when they had slept separately, because Fagan found her alone. In fact, Philip had already left the Palace at six for a distant official engagement.

So, for all his explosions and rudeness, the Queen knows that she can always count on Philip. Not so with other members of the Royal Family, and her job is certainly demanding enough without having to keep at bay a bunch of powerful and often warring personalities. It is, furthermore, a war which has become more intense over the years, as the next generation of the Royal Family has entered the lists.

'The Queen is not good at showing affection'

6 Elizabeth as Mother

Over the course of the last thirty years, the Queen and Prince Philip have been embarrassed, exasperated, infuriated, worried and utterly dismayed by the antics of their wayward offspring. The Queen may be able to compartmentalize her life, but even she cannot put her children and the profound anxiety they have caused her into cosy little boxes; and, from time to time, behind closed doors, her despair pours out.

'I was once with the Queen and Prince Philip during the early 1990s when they spoke very frankly of the desperation they feel about their children,' said one retired courtier. ' "Where did we go wrong?" the Queen asked Philip, "and what can I do now? Charles is already in his forties." She feels the most tremendous guilt about the fact that her work dragged her in other directions, that she has sacrificed her family life for her country.'

Even her most loyal advisers fear that her sense of guilt may be fully justified, and lay the responsibility for the dysfunctional Windsors firmly at their parents' door. The Queen, they argue, may have been presented with a ready-made problem in the shape of her mother, but she and Prince Philip between them have managed to create four problems of their own.

'If the Queen,' said one of her former private secretaries acidly, 'had taken half as much trouble about the rearing of her children as she has about the breeding of her horses, the Royal Family wouldn't be in such a mess now. It's always been all too easy for her to say, "I've got two red boxes full of documents from Whitehall upstairs. That is my constitutional duty, and I'd really rather read them than risk having a row with my sons, my daughter, my husband or my mother!" She didn't spend anything like enough time on the family.'

This, at least, is one issue where courtiers at Buckingham Palace and St James are entirely at one. 'If she'd taken being a wife and mother more seriously, and spent less time reading those idiotic red boxes – and to what effect one asks,' grumbled one of Prince Charles's former private secretaries, 'it would have been far better. Yes, she can handle Prime Ministers very well, but can she handle her eldest son – and which, pray, is the more important?"

As a monarch, the Queen's performance has been well-nigh flawless. As a mother, however, she has often been less than adequate, for much of the time so detached from the lives of her children as to be little more than a distant figurehead, determinedly keeping their needs at arm's length. 'Utterly, utterly lacking, I'm afraid,' said one retired courtier caustically.

Far from giving her children the firmness and guidance they so badly needed at crucial moments in their lives, she did absolutely nothing. In particular, by failing to take Prince Charles under her wing, as both son and heir, she arguably made the future of the monarchy less secure, an astonishing piece of negligence in a woman so inspired by a sense of her own divine calling.

There are those who vigorously defend her against the charge that she was a cold mother in Charles's early years. 'It simply isn't true that she neglected Prince Charles,' said Lady Elizabeth Cavendish, one of the late Princess Margaret's ladies-in-waiting. 'People of my background did have nannies, but I stayed at Sandringham a lot in those early years and she wasn't at all chilly with him. She used to come to picnics where he was the centre of attention, she adored him. The idea of her being a cool mother is nonsense.'

Yet the children of senior courtiers who went to Buckingham Palace to play with Charles and Princess Anne sensed a marked coolness in their relationship with their mother which struck them as distinctly odd; and members of the royal household who spent virtually their entire working lives with the Queen formed exactly the same impression.

'She really had very little to do with Charles,' Lord Charteris told me. 'He'd have an hour after tea with Mummy when she was in this country, but somehow even those contacts were lacking in warmth. The Queen is not good at showing affection. If I were Prince Charles, I'd think my mother had been unfeeling. She'd always be doing her duty, and his father would be rather grumpy, about almost anything. And neither of them was there very much.

'The nannies had a lot more to do with Charles. He had a very good relationship with Mabel Anderson, but it just was not the same between mother and child. He must have been baffled by what a natural mother–son relationship was meant to be like.' The newsreels of the time often show a little boy who looks lost and puzzled as his mother shakes hands with officials rather than holding his.

By all accounts, Charles was a gentle, shy, sensitive, terribly polite child – 'The sort of child,' said Lady Mountbatten, 'who, if he had two sweets, would always offer you one.' He was the sort of child, in fact, who needed warmth, tenderness and approval to help him blossom.

What he actually got, growing up as he did in what one cleric described as 'the most old-fashioned home anywhere in the world', was a tetchy, often disapproving father and a cool, endlessly preoccupied mother with little time or instinct for outward displays of maternal affection.

'She treated Charles very nicely,' recalled a member of the royal household, 'but she was never warm. There were no open arms, no hugs. I can hardly ever remember her kissing him.' Even on holiday, at Balmoral, the Queen's relationship with her son was apt to be cool and considered. Lord Charteris remembers motoring back from 'some heather-growing territory', with the Queen driving, when Charles threw something out of the window.

After a hundred yards or so, she stopped. 'D'you think you'll be able to find that, Charles?' she said quietly, where a less detached parent might simply have either ignored it or told him off. 'I'll try, Mummy,' he replied obediently, and got out. He would have been, said Charteris, about seven or eight at the time.

'I'm afraid the Queen has always been rather cool and distant with her children, I don't know why,' remarked one of her longest-serving ladies-in-

waiting. 'She's certainly not mumsy in any way. The Queen Mother was exactly the same. The Royal Family are just not like the rest of us. Perhaps they become more and more separate from their children partly because they're always surrounded by servants.'

It might be said, by way of excuse, that Elizabeth simply adopted the upper-class and upper-middle-class style of child-rearing current in the 1920s and 30s; and the fact that Elizabeth had come to the throne so young scarcely helped. Any inclination she might have had to be maternal was snuffed out by an avalanche of new duties. Suddenly, this woman of twenty-six with two small children was cast into a world of formidable older men and laden with the all-consuming responsibilities of a head of state with territories around the globe.

'At the beginning,' Lord Charteris once told me, 'she was learning the job and simply had too much on her plate to enjoy Charles and Anne. She went off on a six-month tour just eighteen months after her accession in 1952, leaving the children behind.' Charles would have been three at the time, Anne barely two. To the average modern parent, that seems simply incredible.

'She gave them what was really a terribly old-fashioned upper-class upbringing,' Charteris went on. 'The style had been formed pre-war, it was really a complete time-warp. And, in the years that followed, that kind of family *never* talked about their difficulties. Oh no, what an idea! The Queen, just like her mother, is terribly bad at that. In thirty years with her, it wasn't often that I got her to talk straight about such things. Why? Oh, keeping up appearances, stiff upper lip, *pas devant les domestiques*!'

So, the Queen's children were handed over to nannies and a kind of emotional cauterization took place. Something was sealed off very early in them. For the Queen, that might have been a strength, but the royal children may have felt from the beginning that they were very much on their own.

'As children,' said one of the Queen's former private secretaries, 'I don't think they felt they could talk to her. She's so strong, so stiff upper lip, so afraid of her emotions. They got the message that they were expected to overcome their difficulties for themselves and get on with it.' In an emotional sense, they were latchkey children who happened to live in palaces.

Elizabeth and Philip holding six-month-old Charles.

The Queen was perfectly happy to let Prince Philip become the dominant force in the family but Philip, who had had neither home nor parents when he was a child, therefore had no model in his mind of what a home was like, still less how to create one. He was trying to be a father without ever having had one himself. His own necessarily self-sufficient experience was the only model he could draw upon. He therefore expected his children to stand on their own feet, just as he had had to do. The Queen left the children to Philip and Philip left them to life.

'He took the view,' observed one of the Queen's ladies-in-waiting, 'that it was no good trying to mould them, that the only way they'd learn was by doing it for themselves. Right from the beginning, they were given a tremendously free rein. Even when they were quite young, Charles and Anne did their own thing without any recourse to their parents, and quite soon had their own offices, secretaries and programmes. Both the Queen and Prince Philip seemed rather dispassionate and uninvolved. They usually didn't know what the children were doing.

'If any of them had a problem, they didn't talk it over. They didn't expect to have much to do with each other's private lives. The parents not merely found it difficult to give advice, they didn't even want to be asked. So, because of that early independence, it became more like a club than a family. They didn't have much common ground and they never developed the habit of talking to each other, except about the most trivial things.

'Charles and Anne, in particular, would also have thought, "Don't let's bother Mummy, she's got enough on her plate already." And she wouldn't have expected anything else. No feeling sorry for yourself! Summon up the blood, don't be such a wimp! The Queen and Prince Philip brought up the children very toughly. Never cry when hurt, never make a fuss, never say "that awful engagement!"'

It sounds more like military training than family life, a preparation for an endless assault course of duty with precious little room for normal emotion or human weakness. In all of this, they precisely mirror the behaviour of earlier generations of the Royal Family. Lord Harewood, the Queen's first cousin and grandson of George V, writes that the whole of his mother's family bottled up their feelings and avoided discussing anything awkward. They never, he adds, talked of love or affection and what they meant to each other, but rather of duty and behaviour. He might have been talking about the Queen Mother, the Queen and Prince Philip.

When Charles was a boy, Philip could not have been, in some ways, a more devoted parent. He taught Charles to shoot and fish but, as time went on, began to give the impression that Charles was not the sort of son he had wanted. 'There was always a feeling of antagonism between them,' recalled a member of the Household. 'Philip was always getting on at Charles about something, being niggly about the most minor things.' He could become irritated by even the smallest detail of Charles's behaviour. One of Philip's friends recalls him becoming enraged because he had found his son reading in bed. 'If he wants to sleep,' stormed Philip, 'why doesn't he sleep? If he wants to read, why doesn't he sit in a chair and read?'

Yet Philip's irritation with Charles is perfectly understandable to courtiers and aristocrats who know them both well. They believe that Philip was simply trying to compensate for the insecurity of his own childhood by exercising too much control over his eldest son.

'When they're little, there's no need to worry about making them secure,' explained the owner of a large estate which has been in his family for several hundred years. 'But, when they're beginning to have a mind of their own, you start "doing your best" for them and, if they don't fall in with your ideas, you try to impose your will. There was nobody around when Philip needed someone to guide him and, if you've had insecurity like that, you tend to behave like a super-guide to your eldest son, to bang it in when what he really needs is understanding, to impose yourself upon him even more heavily than a normal father does. And, if he's going to be King, you're inclined to be even more bloody to him. I know Philip quite well and I'm sure that's how it is between him and Charles.'

'Look, I'm divorced,' said a former Palace insider, 'and I know that I want even more for my children to be secure, so I try harder and it can make me pushy, opinionated and domineering towards them. Philip's early insecurity affected his behaviour towards Charles in exactly the same way.'

In any event, Philip came to regard Charles as a rather wimpish, hesitant creature who badly needed toughening up. Princess Anne was far more to his taste. Members of Philip's staff remember Charles as 'a gauche little boy of twelve being overpowered by his sister' as they wrestled together on the ground. When they went go-karting together, it was Anne who drove faster, cornered harder – and won. Anne stood up to her father's bullying, which was exactly what he wanted. Charles simply collapsed.

He was clearly not fitting the mould Prince Philip had in mind. Something had to be done. That something was to send him away to Philip's old school, Gordonstoun, where, from the outset, he seems to have been mercilessly bullied. Writing to a friend at the time, Charles called the school 'this hell-hole'.

He was so desperately unhappy that, after two terms, he pleaded to be taken away. Given the choice, he would have preferred to be tutored by Christopher Trevor-Roberts, a talented teacher who had been recommended by Martin Charteris. The Queen invited Trevor-Roberts to Buckingham Palace for lunch, told him of her worries and those of the Queen Mother about Charles, and asked whether he thought Gordonstoun was the right school for her son. In spite of her apparent coolness and formality, her intervention showed just how anxious she was about Charles's profound unhappiness.

Trevor-Roberts had already tried to get him up to speed in maths – 'picking up Euclid's theorems,' he told me, 'was not his cup of tea' – and discovered that the boy was 'simply not a rough and tumble sort of chap'. In fact, Charles preferred poetry. Trevor-Robert says that he had found Princess Anne, to whom he had taught Latin, entirely different. She had called him 'Trevvy' and, noticing that he always wore the same tie, asked pertly whether it was because he did not have another one.

Over lunch, the Queen and the schoolmaster discussed alternatives such as Eton and Westminster (the Queen Mother favoured Eton) but, in the end, nothing was done. 'Charles did his best to get taken away,' said Lord Charteris, 'but the Queen was not convinced and Prince Philip wouldn't have agreed under any circumstances. It would have indicated that Charles *was* a wimp.' On matters of that kind, the Queen was ready to assume that her husband knew best.

In any case, Philip thought Eton too risky on security grounds, did not like many of the Old Etonians he had encountered at Court and did not approve of what he regarded as the predictable, upper-crust nature of the place. In many ways, Charles had begun to feel no more at home with his own family than he was at Gordonstoun.

'Here is this boy,' said a cleric who knows him intimately, 'who is enormously sensitive, loves poetry and has a deeply spiritual side to his nature – he used to go to confession with an old Franciscan friar in his later years at Gordonstoun – as well as becoming increasingly artistic, yet he's living in a household where he finds little or no response to these longings.

'His mother has a picture gallery, but the last thing she is going to do is spend time gazing at a Botticelli. She may occasionally glance at a Stubbs, with all the horses, but that's all, and she would certainly never choose to listen to Mozart or Handel. So Charles really had very little in common with his family at those deeper levels.'

Only with the Queen Mother did he find natural bonds of that kind. 'My grandmother,' he once told a Gloucestershire friend, 'was the person who taught me to look at things.' She also liked Mozart.

'And what does being brought up in a household like that do to such a boy?' Prince Charles's clerical friend went on. 'A household where there is the formality of a bygone age; where his parents are always talking about duty; where, in any case, he has relatively little contact with them; where problems are never discussed and a gloss is put over everything. The answer is that it makes him unsure what human relationships are all about.'

Long-serving courtiers at Buckingham Palace say that they rarely observed signs of physical affection between the Queen and Prince Philip. 'Only once, in all my years there,' remarked one, 'did I ever bump into the Queen and Prince Philip in a fond embrace. That was the only time I saw evidence of that kind of closeness between them. Would Charles, I wonder, ever have seen any?'

So far as the young Prince was concerned, the best thing about Gordonstoun was that it revealed his high talent for acting. He loved being able to lose himself in a fictional character with fictional relationships. In other respects, too, his time at the school was not entirely wasted, as he showed after being shipped off for a spell at Timbertop, the outback offshoot of an Australian school, Geelong Grammar.

'One part of the routine,' said Squadron Leader (now Sir) David Checketts, the equerry who, with his wife Leila, looked after the Prince there, 'was that small groups of boys went off by themselves and spent weekends trekking in the mountains. Those were damned hard expeditions. Prince Charles had inadequate shoes for that kind of thing and, as a result, developed the most horrifying blisters, the like of which I haven't seen before or since. Everybody thought a pommy Prince would call it a day, but Charles carried on with those expeditions even though his feet were in the most appalling state.' So, in one respect at least, Philip had been right: Gordonstoun *had* toughened him up.

He also displayed the kindness which has been a marked feature of his character ever since. 'He was wonderful with our kids,' Checketts went on. 'At one point, our son Simon had whooping cough and once woke Leila and myself in the middle of the night. When we went into his room, we found Prince Charles already there trying to make him more comfortable.'

In some ways, Cambridge did not suit Charles any better than Gordonstoun. He made no real friends at either place and, at the university, according to Checketts, 'didn't really mix with anybody. He lived for the weekends, when he'd go off to Sandringham or stay with family friends such as the van Cutsems or the Keswicks who lived not too far away. From a social point of view, he could have done a lot more at Cambridge.'

As the years went by, courtiers were astounded at how little involvement the Queen and Prince Philip seemed to have in what their children – and in particular the heir to the throne – were doing. When Prince Charles went off to Australia for a year at the age of seventeen, the Queen had not even bothered to meet David Checketts's wife, in whose home he was to live.

'It says something about the Royal Family's attitude to parenthood,' remarked one courtier, 'that they were quite happy to let David and his wife go to Australia to provide a family situation for Charles without ever having met Leila. I'd never let a child of mine go twelve thousand miles to live with a family without having met the wife. How did they know that she wasn't an alcoholic or a nymphomaniac?'

Later, when Charles was doing a stint in the Navy, they seemed to be equally vague about what he was doing. 'I was once having dinner at Balmoral,' recalled a former senior member of the Household, 'when a telephone call came through from Charles. Philip took it and, when he came back to the table, the Queen asked what Charles had been on about. "He's coming out of the Navy next week," Philip replied. "Oh," said the Queen, "I thought he wasn't coming out till next spring."'

'I nearly fell out of my chair. This was the heir to the throne they were talking about, yet they knew so little about what he was up to, they hadn't any very clear idea of his career structure. I thought it was pathetic.'

Often the children found it extremely hard to see the Queen, even on matters of major moment. 'When Princess Anne and Tim Laurence came to talk to me about getting married,' recalled Michael Mann, the former Dean of Windsor, 'I asked her, "Have you spoken to your mother?" Anne replied: "You know how difficult it is to talk to Mummy about these things. Auntie Margaret always says that the only time to see her is when she's on her own and the dogs are not there – and then she's usually too tired." It took Anne three weekends before she could nail her mother down to a date!'

The fact that the Queen and Prince Philip were not hands-on parents left the field wide open for other hands. 'Charles,' Lord Charteris told me, 'fell under the influence of Dickie Mountbatten and that was not entirely good news,' In truth, it was extremely bad news. At a time when Charles needed to be steered away from self-indulgence, Mountbatten advised him that he ought to sow his wild oats before marrying an unsullied virgin. Even Mountbatten can have had no idea just how widely the royal oats would be sown.

For a young man who was still extremely gauche when he left Cambridge, the torrent of temptation with which the world always overwhelms the heir to the throne was altogether too beguiling for Charles. 'Whatever is most seductive,' said Walter Bagehot, the great constitutional theorist of the nineteenth century, 'has always been offered to the Prince of Wales, and always will be. It is not rational to expect the best virtue where temptation is applied in the most trying form at the frailest time of life.' Throughout the 1970s, Prince Charles lived in a style which amply justified Bagehot's dictum.

'I've often asked myself,' said a former senior courtier who was deeply fond of the Prince, 'what it was that spoiled him. And I've come to the conclusion that, after he'd had such an awful time at Gordonstoun, he suddenly found himself in a world where everybody, and the ladies in particular, had their arms wide open. Instead of the world being at his throat, it was at his feet, and he was ill-equipped to deal with it.

'Of course, it was easy for him to attract women. He only had to raise an eyebrow, or flick a finger, and almost anyone he fancied would oblige. Modest

women, even married women such as "Kanga" Tryon, fell like ninepins, and you'd have needed to be jolly strong-minded not to go to bed with women who threw themselves at you like that.'

'And they'd have thought it such an honour,' murmured his wife, without a trace of irony.

Charles had first met Camilla Shand, the woman who was to play such a significant part in his life, in 1970. She already enjoyed a lively reputation, and Prince Charles had soon embarked on a full-scale love affair with her. Even after she had been married, in 1973, to Andrew Parker Bowles – later the bizarrely named Silver-Stick-in-Waiting as commander of the Household Cavalry – there seems to have been only a relatively brief pause before the affair began again.

At about that time, one of the Queen's senior aides felt that he had to tell the Queen that the Prince of Wales was having an affair with the wife of a brother officer in the Brigade of Guards. 'Some time in 1973,' Lord Charteris told me, 'I let her know that Charles was sleeping with Camilla Parker Bowles, and that the Brigade of Guards did not like it. She made no comment and her face didn't change in any way. What advice did she give Charles as a result of that? None at all, I should think. Yet, if she'd taken a stronger line at that point, things might have been very different twenty years later.' The Queen had failed dismally to take action at a moment which may prove to be crucial to the future of the monarchy.

All that happened as a result of Charteris's revelation was that, from that point on, as a former senior courtier recalled, 'We were warned to *prenez garde* and never to include Mrs Parker Bowles on the guest list for any formal event where the Queen was to be present.'

The Royal Family together at Windsor, 1968. (Left to right: Prince Philip, Prince Andrew, Prince Edward, The Queen, Prince Charles and Princess Anne.)

Those who know the Queen well believe that she would have reckoned that what her son was doing was deplorable but perfectly safe since Camilla was a married woman and that, in any case, the affair would soon blow over. 'The news would not have surprised the Queen at all,' said a senior cleric who served her for many years. 'Her reaction would have been that that was a natural thing for an eager young man to be doing. I can remember her commenting about someone else on another occasion: "If he's got a mistress, so what?" Secondly, she'd run a mile before she'd do anything about it. She'd run to the red boxes instead.' It is clear from all this that the Queen's Christian beliefs fall some way short of puritanism.

Some of Charles's aides were shocked that she did not take stronger action. 'It spoke volumes,' said one, 'that the Queen did nothing about the fact that her son was sleeping with a married woman, when she was the one person in the world who I knew from experience could have done something about it.

'Just before I went on a foreign trip with Charles, I discovered that he had made a date to see a female friend in the country concerned, and in an arrangement so bizarre that he was bound to be found out. The only way I could stop him was to let the Queen know, which I did. I have no idea what she said. All I know is that Charles called off the assignation.'

Yet the Queen was perfectly capable of putting her foot down and bringing her children to heel. 'When members of the family became bumptious,' recalled one former Master of the Household, 'she would sometimes slap them down in public. When Andrew was learning to fly and bragging about how good he was, she said something extremely sharp to him. I won't tell you what it was, I'm sure she never meant it. But he piped down, thoroughly chastened.' She had immense authority with her children. Sadly, she used it far too little.

The Queen and her courtiers were, of course, perfectly aware that Mrs Parker Bowles was far from being Charles's only lover. Those who know him well say that, during the 1970s, the number of his amours ran well into double figures. 'A lot of it was pure scalp-hunting, on both sides,' said a man close to him at the time.

There was one woman, he recalled, who said afterwards that she'd slept with a Mexican bullfighter, and now she'd slept with the Prince of Wales. He, of course, came to think that getting a girl was easy and put it down to his charisma. 'He really was incredibly lucky that somebody didn't blow the gaff,' the aide went on. 'A lot of this took place at private weekend parties in what he regarded as safe houses, but the staff would have known what was going on, and they'd have told the policemen whose job it was to provide security cover. That sort of information would have been incredibly valuable if any of them had chosen to sell it.'

His hosts were a different matter; at that time, the upper-class code included a buttoned-up lip, especially where their royal friends were concerned. The British media, too, was still inclined to touch its cap to royalty and steer clear of distasteful exposés. The Prince had plenty of friends – and sycophants – who were only too happy to provide cover for these activities on their estates. There were a few, altogether more robust, who had the courage to chide him for his self-indulgence, but he brushed their concern aside.

Everybody was at it, he would reply to aides: it didn't mean anything, so why were they being so prudish? Why shouldn't he enjoy himself when women threw themselves at him? After all, his great-uncle David, the Duke of Windsor, had done exactly the same when he was Prince of Wales. And none of the women, the married ones in particular, would dare to come out and say they'd slept with him.

His luck, and that of the minders whose job it was to make sure he did not get caught, held – although everyone in the know at Buckingham Palace was terrified that he would be rumbled. 'All one could do,' said one of those involved, 'was hope for the best.'

From time to time, the tabloids printed portrait galleries of his companions and conquests but, astonishingly, never a photograph of the one who really mattered. Either they did not know or, in those more complaisant times, they were not telling.

In truth, the Prince's friends now say, the liaisons provided him with precious little satisfaction, merely a bogus sense of power. 'His sexual relationships,' said one old friend, 'were pretty superficial, like the Duke of Windsor's.' In the Prince's more thoughtful moments, in his view, these indulgences merely served to deepen his already low self-esteem. The first part of Uncle Dickie's advice had already proved thoroughly unhelpful.

What all this did to a man of deep sensitivity and spirituality who, at university, had gone regularly to chapel, it is hard to imagine. Those who knew him well and were fond of him said that it undoubtedly coarsened him. It certainly did nothing to improve an intermittently volcanic temper. He could descend into alarming, foot-stamping fury merely because a valet had forgotten to put his favourite comb on his dressing-table. 'I can't rely on anyone,' he would rage.

Clerics who have come to know him well believe that this period also created deep internal conflicts. 'Because what he wanted was incompatible with what he had been taught was right,' said one Anglican priest, 'it made him a torn man. It was precisely because of those conflicts that he turned to all kinds of other spiritual outlets to find satisfaction.'

In the mid-1970s, Prince Charles got to know Laurens Van der Post, the South African writer and traveller. On their journeys into the African bush, he was captivated by the way in which Van der Post spoke about the local folklore and religion. Some members of the Prince's staff were not quite so enraptured; they sensed that, for all Van der Post's apparent concern for Charles's spiritual development, there was something bogus about a man who was such an inveterate name-dropper and had a mistress tucked away in the background. A recent biography of Van der Post suggests that their instincts were not entirely wrong.

For the most part, however, the Prince's pursuits were physical rather than spiritual. He hunted regularly and began to play polo more often, not only at weekends but also during the week as well. Unfortunately, his passion for polo sometimes conflicted with his duties and, on one occasion, led to severe embarrassment.

He had agreed to read one of the lessons at the memorial service for the former Australian Prime Minister, Sir Robert Menzies, at Westminster Abbey in July 1978. Instead of coming up to London the previous evening, he decided to stay on in the country to play polo, and come up at the last minute. When he did not appear, aides who had gone to the Abbey tried to reach him by car telephone but were told that he intended to play another chukka.

The result was that he turned up half an hour late. That might not have mattered too much, but he had also failed to register the fact that the lesson he was supposed to read had been changed in the last days before the service. He therefore read the wrong lesson. Menzies's widow Pattie was too polite to say anything, but it was only too clear what everyone thought. 'It was an absolute disaster,' said one of his aides.

It was exactly the same during the 1980s at one of the four-yearly services in the Abbey for the Most Honourable Order of the Bath, an order of knighthood for public servants of which Charles is the Great Master.

The Queen invests Charles as Prince of Wales at Caernarvon Castle, 1969.

'Instead of coming up to London the previous evening, as he should have done,' said one of the senior members of the Order, 'he decided to fly up by helicopter the same morning. But there was fog at Highgrove, so he had to whip up by car, with the result that he arrived half-way through the service. He was not there when we processed into the Lady Chapel, though he was in the procession when we came out. Sneaking into the procession in that way was a slightly rum thing to do. The Queen would never have taken that chance. She's far more professional than he is. That was one occasion when she would certainly had let him know how she felt.'

Those close to Charles in the 1970s observed, as one recalled, 'a growing reluctance to feel that he needed to justify his indulgences. He wasn't off the rails, but he was rocking on them.' If the Queen and Prince Philip did or said anything, it had little effect. Even Uncle Dickie became worried. He told *Time* magazine that his great-nephew was always 'popping in and out of bed with girls'. Then, in 1978, he wrote to Charles to warn him that he could be 'beginning on the downward slope which wrecked your Uncle David's life'. Charles, he feared, was fast becoming a playboy Prince. The rest of the Royal Family, too, had begun to feel haunted by memories of the Duke of Windsor.

Throughout the 1970s, as aides recall, there had been 'endless discussion' about finding 'a real job' for Charles, though, if the Queen and Prince Philip took a major part, it does not seem to have been a decisive one. They left that job to his advisers. The idea that he might become Governor-General of Australia had been mooted by David Checketts as early as 1966. Checketts had even identified a splendid house on 8,000 acres, which would have made an excellent residence for the Prince.

There was equally fruitless talk of Charles spending six months at the Cabinet Office, or being appointed an Ambassador somewhere or other. The Queen's senior aides thought it all a waste of effort, and no doubt told her as much. They felt that being Prince of Wales was enough of a role in itself. In their terms, he was not at a loose end. 'That's the last thing I'd have described it as,' said Martin Charteris. 'Hunting, shooting, polo and fornicating – if that's being at a loose end, I'm a Dutchman!' It certainly beat six months at the Cabinet Office but, as a preparation for the throne, it seemed casual and totally unplanned.

The fact that the Queen and Prince Philip did not take a grip of the situation reveals just how ludicrous it is to speak of the Royal Family as 'The Firm'. Immensely dutiful as they were themselves, they were certainly not making the training of the next chief executive their first priority.

Charles did have one big idea of his own, which led eventually to the creation of the Prince's Trust in 1976. 'He was concerned,' said Checketts, 'about the number of young people who sat around with nothing to do. Why not, he thought, challenge them to use their energy and initiative to help themselves, instead of moping around in cafés? I wrote the initial proposal on the back of a brown envelope while we were on a train.' It was to prove an immensely fruitful idea, which, in the years ahead, would help tens of thousands of young people.

As the Prince passed thirty, though, everything else paled into insignificance beside the big issue: what about *his* issue? How long was it going to take him to get married and produce an heir? Princess Anne had married Mark Phillips in 1973, and already had a son. Why was Charles dallying so long? The Queen and Prince Philip were both beginning to wonder.

Charles had talked endlessly in the public prints about how marriage had to be for ever. Occasionally, he reacted against a sense of being pushed by public opinion. It was very awkward, he told *Woman's Own* in 1975, to get married too young, because 'You miss so much.' Those close to him felt that he was not missing a darn thing.

When he had first met Camilla Shand, he was only twenty-two. At that stage, the idea of marriage did not occur to either of them. Apart from anything else, as Lady Mountbatten put it bluntly, 'One didn't marry commoners or subjects.' Thereafter, candidates for the role of Princess of Wales came and went with alarming rapidity. One or two, including Lady Mountbatten's own daughter Amanda, turned him down. 'Amanda knew from the beginning she didn't want to do it,' said a member of her family. 'She did love Charles, but she wasn't head over heels. If you are, you can take on anything, but that didn't quite happen and so she wasn't prepared to pay the price which becoming Charles's wife would have entailed.'

It was not, however, the availability of suitable candidates which most concerned his friends and advisers. His *attitude* to marriage bothered them a good deal more. What he had to do, Charles explained to one of his aides, was find someone young and of the right calibre, so that she already knew what the role involved. He could then mould her into his way of doing things. But, objected the aide, the person he was talking about sounded more like a blown-up rubber doll or a Labrador than a woman of personality and character. And, in everything Charles had said, he pointed out, he had never mentioned the word love. He did not, Charles retorted bluntly, want anyone who was going to run her own life. That was worrying enough. Seasoned courtiers also wondered how Charles would settle down to monogamy. 'The life he'd led,' Lord Charteris once told me, 'was a very bad preparation for marriage.' The Prince was in an appalling dilemma. Everyone, including his parents, was wondering when he was going to get a move on, yet he was in love with a married woman. What on earth was he to do?

At the end of the 1970s, however, he decided that he had at last found the ideal candidate. Diana Spencer was a virgin, she was beautiful, and close enough to the Royal Family to know much of what would be required of her. She had been born at Park House in Sandringham and had no less than five lines of descent from two previous monarchs, Charles II and James II. Her father had been an equerry to both the Queen's father and the Queen. Nor was she a passive agent in their blossoming friendship: she had made up her mind she was going to catch Charles, whom she met through her sister Sarah. At the age of fifteen, she had already decided that she wanted to be Princess of Wales.

A number of the Prince's friends, however, were aghast at the news that he was thinking of marrying Diana. Three of them – Nicholas Soames and his cousins Lord and Lady Romsey – warned him that he was making a very big mistake. Some courtiers who had known Diana as a child at Sandringham remembered 'an attractive, bubbly child'. Others heartily agreed with Charles's friends that he was doing entirely the wrong thing. 'Diana was a little madam,' said one. 'I knew her from the age of four and I just prayed the marriage would not happen. I disliked her so much that, when I found out from the headmistress that she was going to the same boarding school as my daughter, West Heath, I immediately put her down for somewhere else instead.'

When it became clear to Prince Philip that his son was seeing a good deal of Diana, he wrote Charles a letter which the Prince took as an attempt to bully him into marriage. Those who have also read the letter take a diametrically opposite view. 'I've seen that letter,' one of Philip's relations told me, 'and, in it, he simply pointed out that, with Press fever what it was about Charles's other girlfriends, he needed to bear in mind that this girl was only nineteen, very vulnerable and with a reputation to lose. He added that, if Charles wanted to go on seeing her, he had to think seriously about getting engaged.

'Charles saw this as being bullied into marriage. He kept the letter in his breast pocket and, when the marriage went wrong, he'd produce it and say: "Look what they did to me. I was forced into it." In fact, it was the most charming letter you can imagine from a loving father giving very sensible advice.'

Bullied or not, Charles decided to brush aside the doubters and propose to Diana. He was encouraged by the fact that the Queen Mother and her lady-in-waiting Lady Ruth Fermoy, who was also Diana's grandmother, were not opposed to the match. 'Ruth was always slightly nervous of the idea because she knew that Diana's nickname in her own family was "The Governess",' said a courtier who worked in Clarence House at the time, 'but, that apart, she and the Queen Mother were comfortable with the idea and, because there was no overt hostility from the grandmothers, it was easier for Charles to pop the question. In that sense they provided an incentive for him to get on with it.'

As the engagement went on, however, he began to have doubts. At that point, he turned not to his parents but to his grandmother for guidance and reassurance. 'There came a time,' said a member of the Queen Mother's family, 'when Charles began to feel doubtful about the whole affair and asked his grandmother, "How will I know if I'm doing the right thing?" She said, "Would you mind if Diana married somebody else?" "Yes," he replied, he would. "Well, that's all right then," said the Queen Mother. "You obviously do love her."' Charles may have taken his grandmother's words as a reassuring go-ahead.

Even so, his doubts persisted and grew. Members of his own family, too, realized that, although Diana was only nineteen, she was no pliable ingénue. 'He brought her to lunch when they'd just bought the ring,' said one. 'They'd left it in a box in the sitting-room and we asked if we might see it. "Charles," said Diana, "go and get it!" She didn't even say, "D'you mind?" I thought, this girl is certainly not going to be downtrodden.'

'Everything changed after the ring,' recalled one of Charles's friends. 'It was, "I don't want to see that friend of yours any more, the dog must go" and so on. Diana threw some terrible tantrums. Charles began to think, Is this normal? and got really serious cold feet.'

He had begun to realize that, as Soames and the Romseys had warned him, their two temperaments and interests were impossibly different. Diana had lied through her teeth in telling him that she too loved the country pursuits of which he is so fond. In fact, she hated all field sports. She did not like his friends, she did not like many of his family and she certainly did not like the fact that the country house he had recently bought, Highgrove, was a mere seventeen miles from the home of his long-term mistress, Camilla. She tried to get him to sell it and find something much further away.

Given the chance, Charles would gladly have pulled out of the whole thing. 'Had he been a private individual,' said Lady Mountbatten, 'he would not have pressed on. But, by then, he was too committed. He realized that, if he called it off, it would ruin Diana's future. If the Prince of Wales didn't want her, who would? He went as far as raising his doubts with his father.'

A cleric who knows both men well explained: 'What I understand happened on that occasion is that Charles told Prince Philip he wasn't sure he'd done the right thing. His father, thinking that it was for pre-marriage nerves, told him that he had to make up his mind, that he must either go for it or let the girl off the hook.'

Charles decided to cast aside his doubts and go ahead. 'He'd got locked in,' said one of his closest friends, 'and realized too late that he couldn't get out. He'd have been branded a rotter, a shyster and a ditherer. Anyone with a brain the size of a pea could see how things were when the two of them were asked on television whether they were in love – and he replied, "Whatever love is." It was the most painful thing I ever saw.'

Had it been Camilla by his side, Charles would have answered quite differently. He found it desperately hard to break off his affair with her, and gave her a beautiful bracelet as a parting gift. When Diana discovered this, it merely confirmed what she already sensed – that that was where his heart still lay. She, too, was on the verge of calling the wedding off. Her father, Earl Spencer, aware of the tensions behind the scenes, told the Queen that he was not sure Diana should be marrying.

In these circumstances, it was hardly surprising that, at the ball held in Windsor Castle on the eve of the wedding, Diana looked a desperately unhappy woman. Charles danced with her only once, with Camilla several times. 'I could see,' said David Checketts, who was there with his wife Leila, 'that there was going to be an explosive finish to it all.' Just how explosive, tragic and dramatic, nobody could possibly have imagined.

For some years, the public wallowed in the notion that they were witnessing a fairy-tale romance and marriage. Soon, the House of Windsor had not merely one heir, but two. It seemed as if all the monarchy's Christmases had arrived together.

Sadly, it proved to be an illusion. Charles had never been on the sort of terms with his parents where leading questions might have been asked, and answered. Did either of them ever chide him for his promiscuous behaviour and, when Diana hove into view, ask him bluntly, 'If you're going to marry this girl, are you going to give up that mistress of yours for ever? Are you really sure Diana shares your interests? Does she really like country pursuits and painting? Do *you* really like pop music and London life? I understand your difficulties, but is she really the sort of girl you should be marrying?'

The lines of communication between parents and children in the royal household were far too tenuous for such conversations to be possible; its members were simply not accustomed to speak together about their real fears and feelings; the royal children, almost from the outset of their adult lives, had been left too much to their own devices. In short, the Firm had never become a real family.

'The Queen and Prince Philip had no idea what to do with Diana'

7 Domestic Tangles

In the 1980s, while the going was good, and the media were treating the Royal Family as a delightful and piquant fairy tale (with a few minor foibles), the inherent weaknesses of the Windsors as a family did not seem to matter very much.

The frosts which followed, however, were bitter indeed. As royal marriages fell apart, seedy relationship were gleefully chronicled (and photographed) by the tabloids, and old mistresses were drafted back into service, the young royals looked increasingly like a bunch of immature if glitzy stumblebums. For a time, there seemed to be a new bêtise every other week.

By 1985, Charles and Diana had been sleeping in separate bedrooms for some time. Early in the following year, in desperate need of comfort and consolation, he took up again with Camilla Parker Bowles. Princess Anne and Mark Phillips separated in 1989. In 1992, they divorced and, in the same year, Prince Andrew and his wife separated. Three months later, Andrew Morton's book about Diana revealed the appalling reality of the Waleses' unhappy marriage. The whole royal edifice, which a mere decade before had seemed so reassuring in its splendour and stability, was disintegrating before the nation's eyes; and every episode in that disintegration was chronicled by the media in shameful and lurid detail.

Sadly, the Queen and Prince Philip were hopelessly ill-prepared to help their offspring sort out their domestic tangles. A mother who had not been in the habit of talking to her children about their problems and, indeed, had sought deliberately to keep them emotionally at arm's length, now found that the entire familial landscape from Highgrove to Sunninghill Park consisted of nothing but taut, wounded emotions and apparently insoluble problems. Often, the Queen and Prince Philip seemed to be doing little more than look hard the other way.

The Queen might complain in private that her children were 'rotten pickers' when it came to choosing partners, but had she ever taken the time and trouble to help them pick better? Both she and Prince Philip *were* unremittingly hard-working but, if they did not set aside time to connect with their children, where else did they expect them to find guidance? Given the recent history of her own family, the Queen must have known how difficult it would be for her children to find suitable partners. And if, as toddlers, her children had not felt able to run to her when they were hurt, how could they be expected to start doing so when they had become supposedly self-standing adults?

Staggeringly, she only found time to visit Highgrove, where Charles had created a delightful and stylish home and garden, twice in the first fourteen years after he moved there in 1981. 'To be honest,' admitted one former royal adviser, 'that was quite bizarre.' Martin Charteris explained that the Queen simply could not be fagged to go and that, as the marriage between Charles and Diana became ever more fraught, 'She simply did not want anything to do with that impossible girl.'

So, as Lord Hurd, the former Foreign Secretary, shrewdly observed, the constitutional machinery which the Queen tended so dutifully might be in perfect working order, but 'there was no emotional machinery in place to cope with the situation'. A family starved of any emotional involvement with each other had no reserves of affection to fall back on. Not surprisingly, the end-product of the Queen allowing her children to do their own thing with the minimum of guidance was a collection of individuals running their own shows in what, effectively, were a series of separate courts. With the odd exception, they did not even seem particularly fond of each other.

'There isn't, I'm afraid, a lot of affection between them,' said a retired senior courtier who has spent a good deal of time with the Royal Family at Sandringham and Balmoral. 'The only good chemistry I've ever seen is between Princess Anne and her father and, of course, between Philip and the Queen.

'I suppose it's partly that, if you're royal, you feel a strong obligation to live up to it, to be the great I AM. "I'm the Princess Royal!, I'm Prince Edward!," that sort of thing. You've got to think it, be it and act it all the time. And they don't ever, any of them, want to show any weakness, either within the family or to outsiders. Even after the Wessex PR company disaster, Edward and Sophie in private showed very little sign of being contrite. They were full of bravado. So far as they were concerned, it was everyone else's fault.'

Because of the way they were brought up, in fact, the royal children are living testimony to the truth of Lady Mountbatten's mordant dictum: 'It is more than human nature can endure never to be gainsaid.' According to courtiers who know them well, all four are often unbelievably arrogant, selfish and spoilt. They were never gainsaid anything like enough.

'From their earliest days,' said a former senior courtier, 'the children have been surrounded by people who were terribly nice to them. If there was a cock-up, there was always someone to tell them it wasn't their fault. And they're used to people doing exactly what they want, so they don't expect to be told, "Kindly don't do that!" or "You're doing that wrong." They often take the line, "I *know* I'm right", because they're used to people saying, "Yes, sir, you're the greatest."'

Sometimes their arrogance appalled even the most loyal of courtiers, though, to their shame, they usually did nothing to correct it. On one occasion, Prince Andrew had parked his car close to St James's Palace and, because the police did not know to whom it belonged, they were on the point of carrying out a controlled explosion when somebody told them whose the car was.

Later, over lunch with a group of senior courtiers in Buckingham Palace, Andrew blew his top about what fools the police were. One of those present thought to himself, No, sir, *you're* the fool! but said nothing, and has regretted

it ever since. That, he told me, was typical of what went on; that was what had helped make the Queen's children so spoilt and self-centred.

As the marital carnage continued, the Queen showed herself to be far from judgemental and only too happy to see matters resolved with the minimum of fuss even when the niceties of protocol, to put it mildly, had not been observed.

Her attitude when newspapers revealed that Princess Anne, though still married to Mark Phillips, was having an affair with Commander Timothy Laurence, then an equerry in the Palace, is a case in point. 'When the story appeared in the *Daily Mirror*,' recalled a former assistant secretary, 'most people in the Palace were deeply shocked that a courtier could become involved in that way. One of the definitions of high treason is "encompassing the dishonour of the sovereign's daughter" or something like that. There was a good deal of talk from senior courtiers that Tim would have to go.

'I was quite a chum of his and took the view that if a princess of the blood royal bade you to her bed, you'd be churlish to refuse. I expressed that view to my colleagues and then to the Queen, though not quite in those terms of course. She just nodded and said, "Yes, you know, I've decided I'm not old-fashioned enough to be Queen!" She liked Tim, felt very sympathetic to her daughter and was not horrified in the way the more old-fashioned courtiers were.'

Laurence was told that, technically, he had committed treason and was duly shaken. But since the Queen was only too well aware that he was likely to become her son-in-law, he was allowed to remain. He married Princess Anne in 1993.

The Queen observed the unravelling of the marriage between her eldest son and Princess Diana with sad and helpless resignation. In the beginning, Charles had shown himself ready to indulge Diana's every whim by adjusting the entire landscape of his life. When she made it plain that she did not like any of his close friends, he cut himself off from virtually every one of them.

Four generations: The Queen Mother, The Queen, Princess Diana and Prince Charles with newly-christened Prince Harry.

Out went the Mountbattens, the Romseys, his skiing friends the Palmer-Tomkinsons, the van Cutsems and the eighteen-stone Nicholas Soames, whom Diana described as 'heavy furniture'. Soames, to whom Charles had spoken on the telephone almost every day, was very hurt to find himself in the wilderness for almost two years. The Palmer-Tomkinsons did not see Charles for three. 'The closer you were,' said Lady Mountbatten, 'the more likely you were to be ditched.' Diana even told Lady Fermoy to leave Highgrove and never come back after the old lady had said something she did not like.

'Charles thought that giving up his friends was perhaps the price he had to pay for getting his marriage right,' said one of those who suddenly found themselves persona non grata. 'We couldn't even meet for tea. He thought, "If she feels less confident with these people, I won't see them." Everything which represented something he'd loved had to go. That even included his shooting dog, a Labrador called Harvey.'

Diana also sensed that none of Charles's circle were on her side. 'She thought a lot of them were sycophants, not true friends,' one of her female aides told me. 'Some of them, she knew, hadn't been in favour of their marriage and some were close friends of Camilla. Diana felt she could almost smell Camilla on their clothes. She also felt very insecure because they seemed so smooth and sophisticated. Don't forget that Charles was already thirty-two but going on fifty and that his friends were often older than he was. She, on the other hand, was twenty going on fifteen in some ways, and all her friends were around her own age. She told me, "I can't introduce any of them to Charles because they're so frightened of him."

'So, very soon, she and Charles had nobody with whom to share their lives. I don't think they spent any time finding out what their common life might be. They grew apart before they'd ever had the chance of growing together.'

Prince Charles also had to face the fact that his wife was both ignorant and uneducated to an embarrassing degree. In the early days of their marriage, she telephoned St James's Palace. 'Tell me,' she asked one of her male aides, 'where *is* Dorset?' 'Next to Somerset,' he replied, utterly astonished. Although she unfailingly sent 'thank you' letters within twenty-four hours of having taken part in an event, her spelling and grammar were 'dodgy, to say the least', according to a member of her staff.

Charles therefore, the aide went on, asked his friend Eric Anderson, the headmaster of Eton, who had taught Charles at Gordonstoun, if he could help Diana with the formalities of letter-writing and, in the process, give her some rather more general education. According to the aide, Anderson went to Kensington Palace to give Diana tutorials 'perhaps once a week for between four and six months in 1982'. Once during that time, to her aide's astonishment, Diana rang and asked, 'Could you go and get me some books about the Oxford Movement [the High Anglican pressure group of the nineteenth century]?' You could have knocked me down with a feather but, of course, I went and bought them.'

It was all to no avail. Diana simply did not have either the brains or the application for such complexities; and she was already a deeply insecure and damaged woman before Charles married her. Her mother had deserted her children when Diana was only six years old. According to one of her aides, 'Her parents' divorce left a terrific wobble in her. She appeared to be confident but, underneath, was in constant need of reassurance.'

It was Diana's profound insecurities that, in part, lay behind her frenzied need to control all of Prince Charles's life. 'She said, in effect, "You're mine now, and your life must be wholly shaped around me,"' remarked a retired Cabinet Secretary who observed the way in which the marriage developed. Those profound insecurities were constantly fuelled by a sense that, somewhere in the shadows, an ever-present threat, lurked Camilla Parker Bowles, her husband's one and only true love.

Neither Charles not Diana had been given much clue by their parents about how a relationship such as theirs could be made to work. 'He'd had the glacial example of a mother and father totally devoted to duty,' said one of his friends. 'She'd seen fights and howls and screams of anger, and then her mother going off in high dudgeon with another man.'

One of the Princess's aides totally agreed. 'Charles and Diana,' he said, 'were both very self-centred people. She was used to getting her own way – she had a will of steel – and nobody had ever said "no" to him very much after he left school. He's never really had to think of anyone but himself. Both of them, in my view, were looking for something which the other couldn't possibly provide. He was looking for the mother-figure he felt he had never had, she for a father-figure. That, unfortunately, was a part he couldn't play. He longed to be understood, not to understand.'

The Queen, for her part, had very little to be thankful for in Charles's choice of Diana other than the hope that the two young Princes, William and Harry, would not inherit too much of what a former senior courtier called their mother's 'vain and fickle nature.' 'The Queen was one of the few people who, very early on, had misgivings about the marriage,' recalled one of those who saw a good deal of her at both Balmoral and Sandringham. 'She did not express it directly, she just seemed very cool about it. And when, after some time, Diana took up tap-dancing and started to swim hundreds of lengths in the Buckingham Palace pool, she said to me, "That girl is quite mad!"

'At Balmoral,' he went on, 'where nobody is supposed to leave before the Queen goes to bed, Diana would vanish upstairs as soon as the ladies left the dinner table. Those evenings were torture for her because she didn't have a single subject of conversation, but the Queen resented her leaving in that way. Again, she'd say, "She's mad, she's mad!" I have to add that I hated those evenings too. I used to pray for the Queen to go to bed, so the rest of us could follow suit.'

For a time, Diana went to the Palace fairly often for tea with the Queen, 'partly to have a power base against her husband', according to a former courtier, but then stopped going. The Queen said rather sadly, 'Diana used to come to see me, but she doesn't any more.' It apparently did not occur to her to send Diana an invitation. While becoming ever more critical of her daughter-in-law's behaviour, she would still ask courtiers, 'Are we doing enough to help her?'

As his marriage went from bad to worse, Charles scarcely talked to his mother. His thoughts began increasingly to turn to Camilla. 'Diana at least communicated with the Queen,' one of Charles's senior aides told me, 'whereas he hardly communicated with her at all. And, when he did, he may well have told the Queen a pack of lies about Camilla, so he really didn't behave very well at that time. The Queen had every right to be difficult.'

As the years went by, Charles began to feel desperately lonely. All his friends and confidants had been banished. Diana shared none of his interests. She did not like either Highgrove or Balmoral. She did not like horses, dogs, hunting or shooting. She felt gauche and maladroit at the sort of flamboyant house parties where Charles flourished. He felt like a castaway, cut off from everything he had known and loved. He could not, he felt, expect either sympathy or understanding from his parents. All he would get from them, he thought, was to be told to pull himself together and make the marriage work.

He also became increasingly aware of what he had lost when he had given up Camilla. She had been not merely a mistress, but also a mother-figure; someone who could reassure him, someone who shared his interests, a sponge who could mop up the angst and woe which is a part of his character, but without wanting to possess his soul. It gradually dawned on Charles that he had cut off his life-support machine. 'You wish I were her, don't you?' Diana would say to him. Before very long, he did.

As if this growing sense of loss were not enough, Diana began to upstage him at every turn, to steal the limelight, to make him feel more and more like an irrelevance. When he took the young Prince William to school, there was not a photographer in sight. When Diana took him, there were snappers everywhere. Charles began to realize that he had exchanged a comforter for a competitor.

'The media made such a film-star out of her,' said Lady Mountbatten, 'that poor Charles began to ask himself, "What am I doing? I'm supposed to be shaking people's hands, but I don't think they're interested."' Understandably, he was both humiliated and infuriated. 'He became very resentful and jealous,' said a courtier who knows him well. 'She was supposed to be there to embellish his life, not the other way round. But she'd leapfrogged the monarchy by becoming a member of the new super-class – global celebrity – and that painfully exposed Charles's own uncertainty and insecurity.'

Diana also made the monarchy itself look thoroughly dowdy and out-of-date. Even Charles's greatest supporter, the Queen Mother, observing the way her favourite grandson was being overshadowed by this bird of paradise, remarked resignedly to a Scottish friend: 'Let's face it, people aren't interested in seeing someone in the same suit every week.'

Nor, as their marriage became ever more fragile, did Diana hesitate to rub in the fact that her husband had become nothing more than a supporting player in the royal soap opera. 'It's me they want to see, anyway,' she told him, 'and you know that as well as I do.' For a man with a melancholy, not to say depressive, cast of mind, who needed, as one of his friends remarked, 'to have his fur eternally stroked the right way', this was wickedly undermining.

Diana habitually and deliberately stroked his fur the wrong way. She constantly embarrassed Charles by her wayward behaviour. 'I can remember being at Windsor for a Christmas dinner party in the mid-80s,' recalled a senior

Anglican cleric, 'when she and one of the Queen's equerries with whom she appeared to be in love carried on disgracefully. They were flirting, throwing bread at each other, giggling and shouting, all to Charles's total embarrassment.'

The soul-searing agony of those years helped to turn him into a whinger, almost in the same league as his uncle, the Duke of Windsor. The story goes that, during a dinner party at the British Embassy in Paris, the Duke went on and on about the fact that the Duchess would never allow him to have a new cake of soap, and only gave him the last slivers. 'Why should I always get the slivers?' he whined to his table companions. Prince Charles has never quite reached that standard, but he has often come close.

Early in 1986, he went back to Camilla Parker Bowles and, as a result, Diana usually left Highgrove in floods of tears after her weekend visits, taking the young princes with her. From that time on, according to one of her aides, she often wept profusely on the way to engagements, 'although she never showed it once we got there.' Diana also took out her misery on her staff, whom she sometimes treated with a foul-mouthed harshness that her adoring public would never have recognized.

None of this did anything to improve Charles's own propensity for sudden, towering rages. 'I remember one occasion in 1985,' said a cleric who was present, 'when the Duke of Kent was being given the Order of the Garter, though he wasn't going to be invested as Charles had been. Charles came into the ante-room at Windsor Castle and rushed up to the Garter King of Arms, Colin Cole, shouting, "Why isn't the Duke of Kent being invested? He won't be a proper Garter unless he is!" He had totally lost control of himself. Cole simply replied, "That's what Her Majesty wanted."'

Yet, despite all his domestic anguish, or perhaps partly because of it, Charles somehow managed not merely to go through the motions of royal duty but also to pitch himself headlong into three or four controversial areas of national life. Some of those who have dealt with him frequently say that he only has an average mind, but there was nothing average about the demonic energy with which he tackled a whole range of issues. Again and again, he struck a chord with the public's genuine concerns.

In 1984, he launched a two-pronged attack on architects and the medical profession. Our architects, he declared, had for too long ignored the feelings of ordinary people. The proposed extension to the new National Gallery was typical – 'a monstrous carbuncle'. In 1988, he began planning his own model community on Duchy of Cornwall land in Dorset. In 1992, he set up an Institute of Architecture to train men and women who would fulfil his vision of people-centred development.

As for doctors, he declared, they were far too ready to prescribe drugs for all our ills, far too hostile to anything unconventional. He did not add that the Queen Mother was a great believer in homeopathic medicine or that the Queen herself had been raised on it.

He passionately advocated the merits of the Prayer Book. He backed the then Chief Inspector of Schools, Chris Woodhead, in his battle for a return to traditional teaching methods. He not only created a splendid garden at Highgrove, whose contours he said had come to him in dreams, but campaigned for 100 per cent chemical-free farming. When civil servants, mirroring the Queen's concern that he was becoming too controversial, told him to be careful, he retorted: 'Why should I be careful when I may never be King?'

This firestorm of activity made it plain that Charles, as one of his private secretaries put it, 'is a driven man, a compulsive over-achiever'. Charles felt, as he told one interviewer, that he 'had to rush round doing things and trying to help furiously' or he would not be seen to be relevant.

The fact that his efforts were constantly buried beneath mountains of media trivia about his wife's wardrobe and gymnastic exploits galvanized him into yet more furious activity. He did not intend to become the Invisible Man. While his wife pumped iron in fashionable leotards, he honed his own fitness with every push-up, press-up and trunk-curl in the Royal Canadian Air Force's training manual.

'Prince Charles,' recalled one of his private secretaries, 'half believed it when the papers said he didn't have a real job, and that only added to his determination to do something. He would come out of a meeting and say, "Now you've got to see that the sixteen things we decided actually happen!" "Of course, sir," we'd reply, "but we can't guarantee that the entire population of Toxteth [a part of Liverpool where there had been race riots] will be rehoused within eighteen months." His attitude was, "Why not, you whingeing little halfwit?"'

The Prince's tetchiness, so different from his mother's measured restraint, thoroughly annoyed some senior civil servants. 'With me,' recalled one retired mandarin, 'he was always querulous. It would be: "Why is the Government being so stupid? Why aren't they putting more money into this?" Prince Philip did at least butter you up a bit. Charles just labelled you a bureaucrat and that was that.'

The same mandarin had no respect for the chaotic way in which Charles's own office functioned, so different from the Queen's Rolls-Royce efficiency. 'He wouldn't do his boxes for ages,' he complained. 'He wouldn't work through his in-tray and always left decisions about engagements until the last minute. He'd then decide he'd got a better idea, that he wanted to go to Italy or play polo, so his own staff never knew where they were with him.'

Charles could also appear to be callous. The way in which he provoked others to fire his private secretary, Major General Christopher Airy, in 1991 rather than do the job himself was a prime case in point. On the other hand, there were many occasions when he showed great compassion to those who were suffering. They remained, and remain, secret kindnesses because he would have felt it unseemly to let them be known.

'In 1993,' said a cleric who knows him well, 'Charles was due to go to an official engagement when he heard that Sir Maurice Dorman, a former Governor-General of Malta, was very ill. When he arrived at the house, he found Dorman much more ill than he'd thought, so he cancelled his engagements and spent the whole day sitting by the bedside. Sir Maurice died while Charles was there.'

Similarly, when he heard that a neighbour in Gloucestershire had died, he asked whether he might call on the widow, even though he did not know her at all well. 'She was a lady of the old school who'd been taught that you must never touch royalty,' said one of the Prince's friends, 'but he insisted that she take his arm, and spent two hours comforting her as they walked round the garden together.' Hearing that Lady Hurd, Douglas's wife, was seriously ill, Charles wrote the former Foreign Secretary a long letter and said that he would be only too happy if Judy wanted to come to Highgrove to convalesce.

By the end of the 1980s, Charles's marriage to Diana was plainly in tatters. She was so distraught that, according to her own aides, she would sometimes lie in the flower-beds beneath the windows of Highgrove, eavesdropping on her husband's conversations with friends, in case they were talking about her.

At Buckingham Palace, as one courtier recalls, 'We were all worried sick about the long-term damage this was doing to the young princes.' In 1987, the Queen invited Charles and Diana to the Palace to try to sort out the mess. It was meant to be helpful but, so far as Charles was concerned, it was the last straw. His relationship with his parents was already extremely poor. He had never forgiven his father for sending him to Gordonstoun; he blamed him for pushing him into marriage; now he bitterly resented both his parents for indicating that they held him principally responsible for the failing marriage.

'The horrifying thing,' said one of the Queen's closest friends, 'was that it took them such a long time to realize that the fault was by no means all on Charles's side. My husband and I were so worried that we invited the Queen and Prince Philip to dinner to tell them that Charles had tried desperately to do his best.' But Charles took his parents' attitude as further proof that they had never trusted him, and never would.

As soon as things started to go wrong in the marriage, the Queen Mother, on the other hand, had instinctively taken Charles's side. 'She came to feel that Diana was a very silly girl who had a poor sense of duty, or *devoir*, as she often calls it,' said one of her ladies-in-waiting. 'What she could never understand was that a girl from a good family could have taken on marriage to the heir to the throne without understanding the implications. "I know she's very young," she once remarked, "but she ought to have known better."' As one who had herself taken a good deal of time to consider what belonging to the Royal Family would involve before accepting the Duke of York's proposal of marriage, she felt Diana should have done the same.

And, of course, it was to the Queen Mother that Charles constantly turned for sympathy and help, sometimes in a way that left the Queen less than pleased. 'There was a time,' recalled a senior cleric, 'when Charles did not see Diana for six weeks because they were getting on so badly, and it was to Birkhall and Granny that he ran. The Queen Mother had set high standards of behaviour for her own children but, with Charles, she was far more tolerant of his weaknesses, much to the annoyance of the Queen. She knew her mother was giving Charles a soft time at Birkhall and felt thoroughly irritated.'

According to those who worked for Diana, the Princess herself believed that, when the Royal Family finally came to the conclusion that she had to be ditched, it was the Queen Mother who led the way, closely followed by Princess Margaret and Prince Philip. 'Diana sensed that the Queen Mother saw her as a second Mrs Simpson, who was threatening to undermine the whole show,' said one of her aides. 'She regarded the Queen Mother as a very tough operator who frequently got at the Queen and told her, "Diana is fouling up all you stand for." She felt that the Queen was not strong in family matters, and that the Queen Mother had a huge influence over her in that sphere.' Significantly, clerics who knew the situation at first hand agree entirely with Diana's reading of the Queen Mother's role.

From 1988 onwards, it was clear to everyone, including Diana's own aides, that she was manipulating her children's lives as a way of getting back at Charles for his infidelity. When they were at Highgrove together, she would regularly make a point of taking them to her room for meals, leaving her husband to eat alone downstairs. When he had arranged to take them out, to watch polo or attend a hunt, she would claim that she had already planned something important for them.

'On many occasions,' said a member of her staff, 'she'd use them in ways which were really quite naughty. She'd do things which precluded Charles from being there, and I always wondered why she kept taking them to public restaurants where she knew they'd be photographed. From about 1990 onwards, her whole purpose was revenge, and it totally blinded her to the damage she was doing.'

'Charles would be expecting the boys at a certain time and place,' recalled a member of the Prince's staff, 'and they wouldn't be there. When he rang Diana to find out why, she'd say, "You must have forgotten, I told you they couldn't come because they have to go to the dentist. They can come to polo another time." Now she wasn't a disorganized woman – she used to boast about the fact that she had all her Christmas presents bought and wrapped by the end of October – so it was quite calculated.'

Aides close to them say that the young princes themselves apparently resented being used as pawns in their mother's campaign to wreak vengeance on their father. 'When William and Harry were at Kensington Palace with her,' said another of Diana's aides, 'she often didn't know what to do with them, apart from putting on videos and taking them out for hamburgers – and there are only so many hamburgers you can eat. Sometimes, they'd be left watching films while she went out for the evening. The boys were often bored rigid.'

Because their parents were so bitterly at odds with each other, the young princes were debarred from many things they would have greatly enjoyed. Diana would never allow them to go to the Duke of Devonshire's home at Chatsworth when Charles paid one of his regular visits. Nor could they usually join the stalking parties which Charles organized each year at Birkhall on the Balmoral estate. Since stalking soon became one of Prince William's favourite sports, he felt thoroughly fed up at not being allowed to take part.

Diana even thwarted Charles's desire to send William and Harry to the village schools at Sandringham and Balmoral for the short periods when their holidays overlapped with the beginning of the local terms. In that way, he had thought, they could be brought up to some extent with the children of estate workers. 'But Diana,' he told a friend, 'always wanted to get away from there and rush them back to London.'

In the end, he was driven first to distraction and then to a desire for separation by the way in which Diana constantly whisked the boys away from him. 'I think it all came to a head over the issue of the shooting party at Sandringham in November 1992,' said one of Diana's aides. 'Each year at that time, Charles would invite couples with young children – the Romseys, the Westminsters, the Vesteys, the Nicholas Soameses – but that year Diana said she wouldn't be coming and neither would William and Harry.

'There was a terrific brouhaha, a lot of telephone calls back and forth and that, I believe, was the catalyst which led to Charles asking for separation. He just wasn't seeing enough of the boys, though he adored them. He felt he must have some kind of legal access.' The separation decree took effect in December of the following year.

Diana now became increasingly desperate. All she had, she felt, according to aides, were her body and her boys and she sensed that, slowly but surely, she was losing the boys. 'They'd been exposed to two different worlds,' said a courtier of long standing, 'and they far preferred the country pursuits of Sandringham and Balmoral to her world of Big Macs, Disneyland and yachts.'

In the years before his parents' separation, Prince William had sometimes expressed anger with his father because he so often seemed to upset his mother. As the years went by, however, say courtiers, he began to feel much more at home with Charles, partly because they shared the same enthusiasms. 'William

was wising up to his mother,' said one of Diana's staff, 'and becoming far more critical of her. Much as he loved her, he did not like all her affairs. And sorry though he was about the way the Press harassed her, he also hated the way she played to the newspapers herself. One of the policemen told me that the boys had begun to find more security and comfort in the company of their father and his circle of friends.

'They came to admire their father and to realize that their mother was much more brittle. They also liked the reassurance and privacy of Sandringham, and they liked being with the Queen.'

'When they were much younger,' recalled a former courtier, 'I remember once saying to the boys, "The Queen will be here at tea-time." Harry said, "Who's the Queen?" I was gobsmacked. And I don't think William, when he was much younger, knew she was called the Queen either. She was just "Granny".'

In 1995, at the Christmas lunch for the staff of St James's and Highgrove, Diana slandered Tiggy Legge-Bourke, who had become a mother-substitute for the young princes when they were with Charles, by implying that she had had an affair with the Prince. She walked up to her and said, 'So sorry about the baby,' implying that she had, in some way, lost one whose father was Charles – a total fabrication. When he heard the story, Prince William, who was still being looked after by Tiggy, felt that, this time, Mummy had gone too far. It was not the only time she had gone too far.

Nor was she by any means a flawlessly devoted mother. According to one of those who went with her on private skiing trips to Lech in Austria in 1994 and 1995, she did not even show up for the boys' prize-giving at the end of their skiing course. 'She was on the phone to London,' he recalled. 'She didn't think it important enough to turn up for. When she insisted on going out shopping, even after she'd been told there was a crowd of photographers outside, William did not like it at all. She loved her sons, but only on her own terms.'

The Queen with Sir Robert Fellowes, who advised her on how to deal with the troubled marriage between Charles and Diana. Balmoral, 1991.

Prince Charles, by contrast, was regarded as a thoroughly good father both by the staff at Buckingham Palace and, significantly, by Diana's own aides. 'He wasn't about to change their nappies when they were small,' said one woman, 'but it was very wrong of her to imply that he didn't care about them. William and Harry are the best products of that marriage. The legacy both their parents have left them is horrendous. If they develop into normal, undamaged human beings, it's no thanks to either of them. To hear both their mother and father admit to adultery on television must have been traumatic.'

The separation was nothing more than a half-way house. The years that followed brought only a crescendo of revelation and counter-revelation. Charles publicly admitted adultery in 1994, Diana in the following year. In neither case was the Queen warned of what was coming. She became increasingly anguished: so did Prince Philip. Well might she say, 'Those poor boys, those poor boys.' Well might Philip despair that the Waleses' behaviour was undermining all the work he and the Queen had put into making the monarchy an example to the nation.

The Queen increasingly aired her sense of powerlessness. 'She and Philip were very frustrated at their lack of influence,' recalled a former courtier. 'They were also hugely indecisive on family issues. They didn't know what to do, so they simply stuck their heads in the sand.' In that, they were no different from thousands of other parents whose offspring's marriages were falling apart.

It was left to courtiers, in the shape of the Queen's private secretary, Sir Robert Fellowes, to grasp a nettle which neither she nor Prince Philip seemed to know how to deal with. Getting involved in the Royal Family's marital problems was not the sort of task that he and his colleagues relished. 'I am a private secretary,' grumbled one of them to me at the time, 'not a marriage counsellor.'

The separation of the Waleses in 1993 had already provoked colossal anxiety both at the Palace and in Downing Street. 'What preoccupied those of us who were in the picture,' said a former senior civil servant, 'and that included Robert Fellowes, John Major and people like myself, was the fear that a separation would rebound on the Royal Family as a whole and that people would say, "Diana is the best of you – without her it's not worth having a Royal Family at all."

'Then, when things continued to go wrong after the separation, Robert saw that the boil of a disastrous marriage had to be lanced and that divorce was the best way to lance it. The fact that Diana was his own sister-in-law didn't deflect him from what he believed to be in the best interests of the monarchy. Of course, for at least two years after the separation, Diana was adamant that she would never divorce Charles because she thought he'd just go off and marry Camilla. Then, for some reason, her attitude changed and she came to feel that a good financial settlement would at least make divorce palatable.'

'During all that time,' said one of Fellowes's senior colleagues, 'the Queen and Prince Philip had no idea what to do about Diana. If it had not been for Robert, they'd have *kept* their heads in the sand. Robert told them, "This problem isn't going to go away and there's no point in hoping it will, so we've got to sort it out because, the longer it continues, the more damaging it will be for you as a family and as an institution."

'The Queen is not a leader and, for quite a long time, she and Prince Philip dithered as any family would, but Robert just kept at it. It took him a year or so to persuade them to move. The Queen may have had a strong kernel of belief that they ought to persevere with the marriage. She only gave way after Philip became convinced that there was no alternative to divorce. I think it was Robert who wrote the first draft of the letter which the Queen sent to Charles and Diana.'

'In some sense,' remarked another senior courtier, 'Robert Fellowes was the person who was actually managing the Royal Family at this stage. Particularly in family matters, the Queen is better at following advice than taking the initiative herself.'

'Charles, Camilla and the Queen'

8 Family in Crisis

The end of the Waleses' turbulent marriage was not the end of Princess Diana's impact on the monarchy. In 1997, her dramatic death in a Paris underpass pitched the Queen into the greatest crisis of her reign, a crisis which, for a few feverish days, sent the monarchy reeling. It also subjected the Queen to what Prince Philip regards as her greatest public humiliation, when she felt forced to yield to pressure from the London crowds, fuelled by a hostile media, to come back to the capital before she had intended to.

It was not that she felt overwhelmed either by the Princess's death – far from it – or by the growing hysteria of Diana worshippers in London. 'The idea that she was shattered by Diana's death and the events which followed is as big a misrepresentation as I've ever heard,' said one of her principal advisers at that time. A senior civil servant, asked whether he thought she had suffered an enormous shock when told of Diana's death, found the very idea ridiculous. 'The conception of her having a massive shock about *anything*,' he said, 'is just unreal. She is simply not capable of such a thing.'

The mood at Balmoral when the news came through, indeed, seemed far from distraught to some of those who were there. 'The boys,' said someone who was staying at Balmoral, 'were very calm. They simply busied themselves helping Prince Philip get the food for the usual barbecue picnic. They ate a very good supper.'

The Queen Mother did not seem to be unduly cast down. A policeman on the gate at Balmoral remarked to a visitor arriving at the house that, while children of divorced parents are always pulled into two directions, at least – with Diana gone – the young princes would now only be pulled in one. When she was told what he had said, the Queen Mother simply remarked: 'A very wise comment.'

Prince Charles was riven with sadness and regret and, at that desperately fraught time, turned to his grandmother. 'At the time of Diana's death,' said one of her ladies-in-waiting, 'Charles was living on the edge of a nervous breakdown. Who do you go to at a moment like that – the friend who will always listen and sympathize or the family who don't know how to talk to each other? Of course, he leant on the Queen Mother all the time. On the evening when they were taking Diana's body to Kensington Palace, he spent a long time with her at Clarence House.'

The one thing which did infuriate the Queen was the demand from the tabloid Press that the Royal Standard should be flying at half-mast over Buckingham Palace. 'At tea on the Tuesday,' recalled someone who was present, 'the Queen was obviously very annoyed at being bullied by the newspapers. "The editors know perfectly well why the flag is not flying," she said. "The flagpole would still be bare even if I had died. It *never* flies at half-mast. The trouble is, I've been around too long" – by which she meant that, if she herself had died, everyone would have been reminded of the correct form, that the Standard – by a tradition that goes back well over a century – only flies when the monarch is in residence at the Palace.'

Earlier that same day, she had flatly turned down firm advice form Lord Airlie, the Lord Chamberlain, who was in London and watching the crowds grow ever larger, that it would be prudent to fly the Standard at half-mast. On the following day, with a growing sense among her advisers that the monarchy was in grave danger, she most reluctantly gave way to heavy pressure from all of them, with Robin Janvrin (then her deputy secretary) the most insistent, in favour of half-masting. As a compromise, she agreed to allow the Union flag to be flown at half-mast, but not the Royal Standard.

She was entitled to feel equally angry about the suggestion from sections of the media, and Channel Four in particular, that she had been against sending a royal aircraft to bring Diana's body back to Britain and had wanted it taken to a private place of rest, when that was the exact opposite of the truth, according to civil servants who were closely in touch with events from the very beginning of the crisis.

They say that, as soon as he had heard of Diana's death, Robert Fellowes, with the Queen's full agreement, had ordered that a plane should be sent to Paris with the Prince of Wales, that Diana's body should lie in state at the Chapel Royal and that there should then be a full State funeral. According to civil servants, it was Diana's own family who had initially wanted a private funeral to be followed by a memorial service. As Fellowes told a colleague at the time, 'The Queen and I believe that that is completely wrong and we have managed to persuade the Spencers that what we propose is the right course.'

There was another, far more damaging disagreement that week, the one between Buckingham Palace and St James's. 'What happened,' said a former senior civil servant, 'was that Charles's spin doctors tried to distance the Prince of Wales from the stick which the Royal Family was being given, suggesting that he'd got it all right and they'd got it all wrong. One of the most dangerous things which took place during those fraught days was that the two palaces were totally at odds with each other.'

The Queen's advisers were naturally 'deeply worried' about how she would be received when she arrived back in London. When she was given what one called 'a respectful clap' as she inspected the bank of flowers outside the Palace, they sensed that the crisis had passed.

So Diana was dead, but Camilla Parker Bowles was very much alive and presented the Queen and her advisers with what, in some ways, was an even trickier problem. Little wonder that, in the years which followed, she was less than enraptured with her eldest son. It has proved to be an issue which has not only continued to divide the two palaces, but, for a time, also split Buckingham Palace itself into two factions.

Fellowes's firm conviction was that the Queen ought not to receive Mrs Parker Bowles who, as he knew, had not been considered for any guest list for over twenty years, since the Queen had discovered that Charles was sleeping with her. One of her closest long-serving advisers told me that he had *never* seen Camilla inside a royal residence in his life and that the Queen had never met Camilla 'on her own terms', as he put it, in his time at the Palace, though they might have seen each other at a cocktail party or on a racecourse. Fellowes was also convinced that it would be easier for everyone concerned if the Prince of Wales were to stop seeing Camilla altogether. He indicated as much to Charles. 'He took a very strong line,' said a colleague, 'because he believed that, at that time, Charles's association with Mrs Parker Bowles was endangering the future of the monarchy, and that it was therefore his duty to give her up. His view, I believe, had a considerable influence on the Queen.'

To Fellowes, who regarded himself as a friend of Camilla, whom he had known for many years, it was not a personal matter. 'He discussed the issue at considerable length with the Queen,' said a former senior courtier, 'and came to the conclusion that she believed it would not improve matters if she were to receive Camilla, because she would then be seen as part of the Royal Family.

'That would progress the whole business in a way which suited none of the interested parties, including the Government and the Church of England. It would, they both believed, be like pushing a bus with no brakes towards a precipice, because the media were bound to hype the fact that the Queen had received Camilla. Once they had hijacked the situation, you never knew where it would end.'

At that time, a courtier who strongly supported Fellowes's point told me: 'The Queen cannot understand how the Prince of Wales has become involved with a woman like Mrs Parker Bowles. When asked whether she would receive her, she replied, "Why?" On this issue, the Head Lady is not for turning. She has rehearsed all the constitutional and legal arguments with Robert and knows she can block the Prince of Wales from getting married. To her, he either becomes King and puts Camilla aside, or marries her and reconsiders his future.' It sounded uncannily like Baldwin's view of the choices before Edward VIII.

Fellowes has always maintained that he never took a position on behalf of the Queen unless he was absolutely sure that those were indeed her views, but his critics – both then and now – wonder where precisely those views originated. Was he, they ask, the one who put them into the Queen's mind in the first place?

There were certainly a good many senior courtiers who strongly disagreed with him about the best way to deal with the Camilla issue, by no means all of them in the Prince of Wales's camp. Mary Francis, a former civil servant who had become the Queen's assistant private secretary and who did not get on particularly well with Fellowes, was known to believe that it was no business of the Queen's private secretary to be advising Charles about his relations with Camilla, still less indicating that he ought to give her up. What Charles was doing, she pointed out, was happening all over society. Far better for the Queen's advisers to employ their energies in helping the Queen build a better relationship with her eldest son.

Robin Janvrin, Fellowes's deputy, held roughly a similar view while David Airlie, the Lord Chamberlain, also felt that the Queen should be more sympathetic to Prince Charles, given that the idea of partners was now a recognized vehicle for relationships.

Mark Bolland, Charles's able spin-doctor-in-chief, was fully aware of these differences between the Queen's senior courtiers and, since he took the view that on the family front she is wholly guided by advisers, could not wait for the day when Fellowes, who had banned him from his meetings because he felt Bolland would only leak what was said, was succeeded by the more sympathetic and emollient Janvrin.

Both Bolland and his princely master believed that, if Janvrin could be persuaded to meet Camilla, the Queen was sure to follow. Prince Charles, indeed, was so eager to recruit Janvrin to his cause that he tried to sandbag him into meeting Mrs Parker Bowles even before Fellowes had actually left Buckingham Palace. When Janvrin was visiting St James's Palace one day about a new royal appointment, Charles said to his secretary, Stephen Lamport, 'Camilla is here in the building, why don't we get Robin to meet her?' Lamport duly buttonholed Janvrin, but was told that he could not possibly do it without the Queen's express permission.

A few months later, however, after Fellowes had departed for a job with Barclays Bank, Janvrin duly met Camilla – and at his own instigation. He had obviously made a point of asking the Queen for permission to do so. The issue was so delicate that, for a time, Janvrin did not even tell some of his senior colleagues that he intended to meet Mrs Parker Bowles. When I told one of them what had already happened, he was astounded.

'What happened,' recalled one of Prince Charles's senior aides, 'was that Robin told us he'd like the meeting to take place. He and Stephen Lamport then decided that it would be better if it wasn't at St James's. They thought it would be rather odd for the Queen's secretary to be meeting the Prince's mistress in one of the Queen's own palaces. Camilla also wanted it to be somewhere less controversial.

'So Stephen had the brainwave of asking her and Robin to have a cup of tea in his own home. True, it was still a grace-and-favour house which belonged to the Queen, but they both felt more comfortable with that. They spent an hour or so together and they've met at least half a dozen times since then, at Highgrove and elsewhere.' Thus did a new private secretary completely change the angle of the Queen's approach to the Camilla issue which, after all, was (and is) crucial to the future of the monarchy.

Before long, the Queen followed where Janvrin had led. Early in June last year, she decided to go to King Constantine of Greece's sixtieth birthday party at Highgrove, knowing full well that Camilla would be present. When Constantine told Charles that his mother would be coming, the Prince did not believe it until he had spoken to her himself.

It was just as big a surprise to senior courtiers at Buckingham Palace. 'Robin went up to see her one morning as usual,' recalled one, 'and, when he came down again, he just said, "The Queen's going to Highgrove!" It was a bolt from the blue. She hadn't discussed it at all with us. Robin had worked away at it and said that, at some point, she ought to meet Camilla. After she had said she would, he looked both surprised and pleased.'

According to the senior men at St James's Palace, the Queen had come under increasing pressure at least to meet Camilla both from members of her own family such as her niece Lady Sarah Chatto – 'who was very noisy with her about it' – and from courtiers such as David Airlie and Sir Michael Peat, then master of the Queen's finances, now Charles's private secretary. Janvrin would have told her that the public mood about Camilla was becoming ever more favourable and that, in the light of that, being seen as the hard-faced woman who refused even to meet her eldest son's long-term companion was simply disastrous public relations.

Camilla herself was terrified by the prospect of meeting the Queen and, afterwards, even Prince Charles's spin doctors had to admit that it had not proved to be a 'wonderful to see you after all these years' kind of encounter, that it represented 'merely a cracking of the ice rather than a breaking of it'. The ice, it seems, was still not for melting.

The Queen, however, viewed her trip to Highgrove as rather more than a damage limitation exercise. She also saw it as a gesture which was vital to any hope of building a better relationship with Prince Charles. 'She still feels that he has put his private interests before his duty,' said a former senior courtier, 'but before she acknowledged Camilla, he wanted nothing to do with her, and she wanted nothing to do with him and his new life.

'Before she went to Highgrove, the fact that she couldn't accept that long-term partners are OK these days coloured her view on everything – and since she believes that the succession to the throne must take its natural course, she had to find a way of becoming closer to her son.' She will also have realized that the men at St James's Palace now holds almost all the trump cards, since Prince Charles and then Prince William represent the monarchy's future.

'So,' the courtier went on, 'we cooked up this idea of the Queen "acknowledging but not accepting" Camilla. And it's true that their meeting at Highgrove was very brief, very formal. It was not a close moment, but the Queen had done what she had to do simply by being there.'

Before she decided to go to Highgrove, she would also have known that Camilla's position had taken a turn for the better on another front of considerable importance to her as Supreme Governor of the Church of England. To Camilla's own astonishment, she had already been paid several visits by the Archbishop of Canterbury, George Carey, sometimes accompanied by his wife Eileen. 'No doubt,' commented an Anglican bishop, 'George thought he'd better form a relationship with someone he might have ended up marrying – or at least blessing.'

'The Archbishop pressed to see her,' said one of Prince Charles's aides. 'It was never the other way round. He told Stephen Lamport that it was his pastoral duty. He's met Camilla at her country home, Ray Mill, and here

at St James's. When she asked Charles what she ought to do about Carey's approach, he told her to give it a whirl.

'Camilla is not very churchy and roars with laughter at the suggestion that she is becoming more spiritual. She would never talk to Carey about things which are too close to the bone – her feelings about the Prince, their future and so on – because she was told not to trust him on things like that. She thought him odd but sweet, quite a flatterer. She was charmed by his interest.'

'George's form of religion wouldn't appeal to her at all,' said a senior cleric who knows both Charles and Camilla well. 'He's very much the happy-clappy evangelical, whereas in her mind it's a sort of duty, the aristocratic notion that God exists and that you should have the same allegiance to Him as you do to the Queen. Even so, it does at least give some kind of Christian appearance to things.'

Whatever took place, the Archbishop will presumably have reported to the Queen on the outcome of his 'pastoral' visits. She, in any case, is fully aware of the current attitude of most senior Anglican bishops towards the prospect of Charles remarrying. 'I think there would be a mixed reaction,' said one of the shrewdest of their number. 'The vast majority of bishops would be pastorally positive, but there would be some who'd make biblical noises.

'George himself might feel fairly negative but, because of events in his own family – after all, he blessed the marriage of one of his own children who'd been divorced – he'd say reasonably positive things. Richard Chartres, the Bishop of London, who is close to Charles – they knew each other at Cambridge – would have a rather complex view but, in the end, he'd say, "Yes, providing you keep it low-key."

'I'd give it four or five years before Charles and Camilla want to marry,' the bishop went on. 'By then, the Queen Mother, who doesn't like the idea, probably won't be there and we'll be beginning to think of the end of the reign. If the Queen gave Charles her permission, both George and Richard Chartres would have to do what she wanted because, like all diocesan bishops, they've taken a vow to be her liege-lords and serve her with life and limb.'

The Queen and Prince Philip inspecting the floral tributes to Diana outside Buckingham Palace.

When I bumped into Chartres outside the House of Lords about a year ago, he made a point of saying that he had been very cautious and had not, at that stage, met Camilla.

The Queen may not have changed her mind about Mrs Parker Bowles – she recently remarked to a friend that 'She does look rather worn' – but accepts that she is a permanent feature of the landscape. 'Charles and Camilla,' said a cleric who has seen a good deal of both of them, 'have made up their minds that they are going to spend the rest of their lives together. The Queen realizes that she is a constant and faithful fixture. And Prince William has taken to Camilla with total ease and acceptance.

'There is the root of something good in Charles and Camilla's relationship if it is allowed to grow. But I do actually believe that, for the moment, he and probably she would rather leave things as they are. She loves to have people in her own home rather than trooping around with "Good morning, Ma'am" all the time. And Charles would never tell his mother, "I'm going to marry her." If she said no, he would not.'

The Queen's eldest son has posed endless personal and constitutional problems for her. There is no doubt that she is fond of Prince Charles and that they are now getting on somewhat better than they did, but theirs has never been a close relationship. 'I have never seen any sign of closeness between them,' said a former courtier who has known the Royal Family well for thirty years. Astonishingly, according to one of Charles's aides, it was Lord Shelburne who delivered the invitation to the Queen to attend the Prince's fiftieth birthday party at Highgrove. Charles, presumably, did not ask his mother himself because he was afraid she would decline, knowing that Camilla Parker Bowles would be there. He was quite right.

According to courtiers who know them both well, the Queen thinks Charles is clever and talented, full of enthusiasm but all over the place, slightly dotty, sometimes totally exasperating. She simply does not know how his mind works. In that, at least, many parents will recognize their feelings about their own sons. 'She loves him,' said one of her former senior advisers, 'but she can't understand why he doesn't show the same steadfastness as she does. She thinks he is full of self-pity. She also feels that he makes too many controversial speeches.

'And she does not approve of the fact that, in private, just like his father,

Charles fulminates about Britain – the short-sightedness of our politicians, the so-and-so trade unions. "This bloody country," – I've heard them both say it. So the Queen is genuinely perplexed by her son.'

'She also thinks he is very extravagant, which she isn't,' remarked another former courtier. 'When he was coming to Sandringham with Diana once, I can remember her saying, "He has to have eight rooms!" – including two bedrooms even in the early days of his marriage because he snores, a dressing-room *and* another room where he can write his letters. The amount of kit and servants he takes around is grotesque.

'She also can't get over the way that he makes very senior and busy people trek out to Highgrove all the time because he doesn't like London. She once said, "I suppose it's my fault because I told him never to live over the shop as I've done because you never get away from it," but she does find it stupefying.'

'Comparing herself to Prince Charles,' one of the Queen's former assistant private secretaries recalled, 'the Queen once said to me, "I'm quite an executive person." One of the things she disapproves of in him is that he is not as good as she is at taking decisions and dealing with day-to-day business. Papers go from his secretary to Highgrove and stay there for two or three weeks.'

There have, apparently, even been times when she was ready at least to contemplate alternatives to the prospect of Charles succeeding her to the throne. In the dark days after the divorce from Diana, one of her senior advisers felt that the situation was coming to the point where it might be better if Charles were to retire to the country, marry Camilla and pass on the succession directly to Prince William.

His view was duly reported to the Queen, who, he says, did not react violently against it and, indeed, wondered if it might not offer a possible solution. The adviser eventually changed his mind and came to believe that Charles would, in fact, make a very good King, but the Queen's apparent willingness to entertain the notion is revealing.

There is hurt and bitterness on both sides. The Queen was deeply wounded by Charles's not-so-veiled attack on Prince Philip and herself in Jonathan Dimbleby's authorized biography *The Prince of Wales*, in which it was clearly implied that she had been a rather cold mother and Prince Philip

so brusque as to be a bully. She also profoundly disapproved of the way he drifted back to Mrs Parker Bowles as his marriage fell apart. Charles is furious that the Queen has never, in his view, adequately acknowledged the primacy of his position among her offspring and, too often, treats him no differently from his brothers and sister.

'In some ways,' said one of his aides, clearly reflecting Charles's own view, 'the Queen has behaved as if she is the only one who matters. She has not planned for the future very well, she almost seems to see herself as the last sovereign. Everything has been about what was good for her, not what was good for the monarchy in the long term. His resentment comes from not being allowed to be involved enough, a feeling that his mother has treated him no differently from his siblings. He can't understand the total absence of motherly genes in her. He feels that she doesn't really like him.'

A large part of the problem is Charles's exceptionally poor relationship with his father, whom he does not know how to handle, though his response to Philip's often hectoring manner is more robust than it was. Even with clerics he totally trusts, he finds it impossible to talk about his father.

'Charles is quite frightened of his father, who dominates the family by being bullying and loud,' said one of the Prince's aides. 'He deals with it by disengaging. That is why he doesn't play a bigger role in family affairs. His father often doesn't let him get a look-in, but Charles is sensitive – far too sensitive.'

'For some years,' said a man who sat with both of them on the Royal Estates Committee, 'Charles was virtually a silent partner. If he said something, his father was rather apt to jump down his throat. The trouble is, they're so completely different in judgement, style and outlook. Charles always wants to turn the clock back – he's all for lovely Victorian loos and old barns – whereas Philip is always looking towards the future.' The two men have very different ideas about how the monarchy should be run, as witness their furious dispute about whether, and on what terms, Prince Edward and his wife Sophie were to be allowed to continue with their film and PR businesses – and the Queen is often caught in the

A public kiss: Prince Charles and Camilla Parker Bowles in June 2001.

middle. According to the former Dean of Windsor, Michael Mann, 'she is constantly torn between loyalty to her husband and her son'.

'Charles never says, "I hate Mummy,"' said a frequent visitor to Highgrove 'but he tells a lot of Mummy stories which are not very kind to her. He'll take you round the house and say, "That's a piece of furniture I rescued from Buckingham Palace," with the clear implication that his mother and Prince Philip are philistines. He once said to me, "Prince William was rude to his grandfather and I had to correct him, but my heart wasn't in it!"

'I was once invited to Buckingham Palace for lunch and not long afterwards we were summoned to Highgrove because Charles was longing to know how bad it was. When I told him what it had been like, he said: "They have no idea how to entertain. Why do they put people through that torment?"

'Charles is absolutely desperate for his mother's approval and knows he'll never really get it. He's the wrong sort of person for her – too needy, too vulnerable, too emotional, too complicated, too self-centred, the sort of person she can't bear. Arts, charitable causes but unwrapped in a rigid sense of duty, it's all anathema to her. To his dying breath, he'll want her to say, "Well done, Charles," and *really* mean it – and he's afraid she never will.'

Charles's own aides entirely agree. 'Forget about Diana and Camilla,' said one. 'The lack of approval from his parents is the be-all and end-all so far as he is concerned. It is all down to Mummy not saying, "Well done," and Anne and Edward being the favourites.'

Two of the Queen's other children – Anne and Andrew – made wilful, subsequently woeful marriages which failed, and the tale may not yet be fully told. Prince Edward and his wife Sophie have already caused her considerable embarrassment. The Queen had an extravagant mother; she had a sister whose theatrical amours and antics once provoked her to snap to Lord Charteris that Margaret was 'living in the gutter again'; and her husband, though wonderfully supportive, can often be domineering and difficult.

Nor have the family become more benign as the years have gone by. The war between Philip and Charles rages on. Charles loves his mother but nonetheless believes that she is ruled by her husband. And the Queen sees less of Prince William than she would like.

Compared to dealing with that little lot, doing her job as monarch must have seemed to the Queen like a piece of cake. For the most part, moreover, given her profoundly dutiful nature, it has been a piece of cake she has relished.

'She is formidable . . .
It's because there is such
natural worth in her person'

9 Head of State

The Queen has spent her working life in a heavily male environment. Her senior courtiers have almost all been men. The senior politicians and civil servants with whom she has had to deal have, with one or two notable exceptions, been men. Even two of her principal leisure pursuits – racing and shooting – take place in what is a largely masculine world although, in the case of shooting, she performs what might be thought of as a feminine role.

It is, therefore, hardly surprising that, in some ways, the Queen's job seems to have unsexed her. 'There is a certain manliness to her,' remarked a former courtier. 'She displays a lack of sensitivity, a toughness. That's not really surprising because she's been dealing with matters of State all these years and they are not, by their nature, feminine issues.'

Those close to her say that she not only stands like a man, she also thinks like one. 'A woman's mind,' observed a former member of the Household, 'tends to revolve on wheels of emotion, a man's on calculation, and I think the Queen's mind moves on wheels of calculation.'

She normally gets on well with men. Women are quite another matter. As one courtier put it: 'The hierarchy of what she feels most comfortable and happy with is dogs, horses, men, women.' Children apparently do not come into the frame at all. Just how uncomfortable she can be with members of her own sex is obvious from the positive cannonade of disappointment and complaint which comes from women who have met her.

'She's absolutely hopeless with women,' declared the wife of one former Master of the Household. 'She has no idea how to take a conversation forward.' Sometimes, indeed, the conversation never begins at all. A lady who is the head of a think-tank was invited to lunch at Windsor with her husband. 'She came away shattered,' said her friend, Lady Rees-Mogg, 'because the Queen did not address a single word to her. She was treated as merely an appendage of her husband.'

'My wife thinks the Queen's bloody rude,' exploded a former courtier. 'We were invited to Windsor for a fun evening. After dinner, the Queen said, "Now, we can either play charades or watch a film." So my wife said a film might be enjoyable. "Oh well," said the Queen, "we're playing charades." Why ask the question if you've already made up your mind? There's a kind of disregard of women and their opinions.'

Even ladies with considerable social skills find the Queen extremely hard going. 'I think she's genuinely shy,' said one of the Queen Mother's ladies-in-waiting. 'I know she's marvellous with dogs and horses, but it really is hard work to sustain a conversation with her if you have no views about vets and flea collars!

'After church at Balmoral, you always go back to the house for drinks to meet the clergyman and the weekend guests. On one of those occasions, I walked into the room and found the Queen standing there alone without an equerry. She looked at me and I could see in her face the thought, "What am I going to do now?" She is quite incapable of stepping forward and making light conversation. She has absolutely no small talk.'

He had not yet met a woman, commented one of Prince Charles's former private secretaries, who had found it possible to have an easy, flowing conversation with the Queen. In that sense, she is just like the great legion of men who have no idea how to talk to women whom they meet at lunch and dinner parties.

The same level of unease in dealing with women is evident even in her role as Head of the Commonwealth. 'She was far more formal in dealing with Mrs Bandaranaike, Indira Gandhi and Eugenia Charles of Dominica,' recalled Sir Sonny Ramphal, the former Secretary-General. 'There were very few male heads of state where there was that degree of formality.'

Nothing illustrates the Queen's maladroitness in dealing with members of her own sex than her encounter with a woman who is a considerable celebrity in her own field and was invited to one of the regular lunches for the great and the worthy at Buckingham Palace.

'Before the Queen arrived with the Duke,' the woman recalled, 'the Master of the Household came up and told me, "Her Majesty will speak to you before lunch but not thereafter," which scarcely seemed to promise a joyously relaxed occasion. Then there was an explosion of dachshunds and corgis, followed by the Queen in a hyacinth-blue dress.

'There was another, rather large, female guest, whom I mentally nicknamed the Human Mountain. The Master of the Household presented us both to the Queen and the Queen just nodded. Then she was brought a drink on a tray and she stood there – she just stood there!

'So I said, "Your Majesty, I'm pleased to see the dachshunds, my mother has had them all her life." Without looking at me, she just said: "Oh!" So I tried again and asked whether she was pleased with the restoration of Windsor Castle. "Yes," she replied. Then I made my final effort: "But you don't feel the spirit of the place has changed?" "No," she said. She had a few words with the Human Mountain and moved off.

'I glanced at the Queen a lot during the lunch and, for a good deal of it, she said nothing. She looked with a completely fixed expression at the table beyond her plate. I felt I couldn't exercise my normal social skills, that it wasn't my place to, but we were given less than no lead. The Queen looked thoroughly bored, but the thing which really struck me was the unmistakable unfriendliness.

'At about twenty-five minutes to three, as we were having a drink after lunch, the Master of the Household told us that the Queen would be leaving shortly, so we all flattened ourselves into a respectable crocodile. None of us said, "Thank you," as she went out, we just stood there and she didn't say a word to any of us. I went there feeling like a loyal subject, not a citizen, but she

didn't make me feel like one. When I left, I just wanted to cry. I felt worn out, disappointed, jangled up.'

I thought perhaps that the Queen had been having a bad day but, when I told the story to a former Master of the Household, he nodded and murmured: 'Her experience is not untypical.' An even more senior courtier remarked, by way of explanation: 'Women's talk simply doesn't interest the Queen, she likes men's talk. Chatter-chatter, that's when she clams up. She's interested in things that matter.'

When she is dealing with men and things she *does* think matter, she is often remarkably easy to deal with. A few years ago, a Permanent Secretary at the Welsh Office who is by no means a card-carrying royalist was summoned to the Palace because the Queen felt she needed a briefing about the Principality. 'I turned up feeling quite nervous,' he recalled. 'When I'd met her previously at receptions, she had struck me as very correct and quite cold, but this time I had the most enjoyable forty minutes with her.

'She had some funny things to say and, when I started making jokes, she laughed a lot. I thought, "Gosh, she's warm, pretty and clever!" After five minutes, I stopped being guarded. I'd not called anyone "Ma'am" since I left primary school and at no point did I say either "Ma'am" or "Your Majesty". She wasn't in the least put out. It was a very relaxed and friendly occasion.'

That, no doubt, is one reason why a succession of Prime Ministers have both valued and enjoyed the weekly audience with the Queen, this extraordinary ritual which brings together the most powerful citizen in the land and a head of state who, on the face of things, has scarcely any power at all. There is about that occasion just the faintest whiff of the factor going to the big house to give an account of his stewardship.

Lord Howe, who went to the Palace several times as Chancellor to tell the Queen about his budgets and often travelled abroad with her as Foreign Secretary, speaks about 'a pervasive aura of deference' when dealing with the Queen. Even the highest-ranking Cabinet ministers feel humbled when they are expected to stand in line in some overseas capital waiting for her to arrive.

'She is the only person in the whole complex of government to whom the Prime Minister can talk frankly knowing that their meeting is totally secure,'

En route from Buckingham Palace to the Opening of Parliament, December 2000.

said a civil servant who served three Prime Ministers as private secretary. "She has such a depth of experience and knowledge that she is bound to have things to say which are worth hearing.'

When he went to the Palace in 1980 to tell the Queen about his first Budget, it struck Geoffrey Howe very forcibly that 'it might be my first but it was her twenty-eighth and I was her twelfth Chancellor of the Exchequer'. And that was twenty years ago. The Queen had been on the throne for a year before Tony Blair was born.

The arrangements for the audience are simply enough made. 'The way it worked in practice,' said one Prime Ministerial private secretary, 'was that I would tell the Queen's private secretary each week what the current concerns of the Prime Minister were, and he would let me know what she wanted to hear about. The Queen had her own way of letting her views be known before they actually met. Half a dozen times during my years at Number Ten, her secretary told me, "This is what the Queen thinks," with the clear understanding that I would pass it on to the Prime Minister.

'But they didn't always follow the agenda we'd set out. When he came out of an audience, Jim Callaghan would sometimes say, "Well, we didn't talk about any of that!" Neither he nor the other Prime Ministers I served ever told me what *had* passed between them and the Queen. I didn't ask and they didn't say.'

In this age of the all-pervasive leak, it is an eighth wonder of the world that what was said in those audiences has never been revealed. If a decision is taken which requires action by either side, then the private secretaries are told, but beyond that all is silence. 'We'd ask what the Queen and he had agreed,' said one Prime Ministerial aide, 'but we were never given anything like a verbatim account.' The room in which the audience is held is swept for 'bugs' three times a year.

None of the Downing Street officials to whom I have talked have any doubt that their masters greatly valued their time with the Queen. 'I know from personal experience,' said Lord Armstrong, who served both Harold Wilson and Edward Heath, 'that there were at least two Prime Ministers who came away from audiences impressed by what the Queen had said – and taking it seriously.'

'The value of it,' said a man who worked for three Prime Ministers, 'is that it enabled them to explain the issues they were dealing with to a woman who is completely discreet, who is not an inferior and who has heard a very great deal in her time. It is not in any sense a debate about policy. I can't imagine a Prime Minister in one of those audiences saying, "I'm thinking of handling it this way," and the Queen replying, "I wouldn't if I were you."

'He might say, "I'm having a terrible time with Mugabe," and she might say, "I know it's awkward but . . ." One effect on policy is certainly that any Prime Minister would hesitate to neglect the Commonwealth, because he'd know that he might have a frosty time with the Queen if he did!

'But whoever the Prime Minister is would find that there are a great many things she doesn't have views about. When you sit next to her at dinner, you can perfectly well have a conversation about devolution but I can't imagine discussing hospitals or schools with her. Politically, the Queen comes from the bored centre. What's she interested in are things going on as they are, tolerance, good manners, Christian behaviour, doing the right thing.'

'For any Prime Minister,' said Lord Owen, the former Labour Foreign Secretary, 'making weekly visits to the Palace is a tremendous deterrent against shabbiness and sordid actions. Politicians are prone to cut corners, do deals, behave badly. In some way, they seem to become better people when they are Prime Minister and I firmly believe that the Queen's relationship with them is a factor. If you have someone senior to you whom you respect and who may know more than you realize, it has its effect. It may be hard to tabulate the Queen's influence but, in my view, it is a very important safeguard, a fail-safe mechanism.'

'She is formidable,' agreed Lord Waldegrave, the former Tory Cabinet Minister. 'I've been shouted down by Mrs Thatcher and it was very unpleasant, but I'd much rather have that than the Queen's disapproval. I wouldn't want to face those eyes and those folded arms. Why? It's because there is such natural worth in her person.'

All ten of the Queen's Prime Ministers set sufficient store by their audiences that they made a point of going to the Palace both promptly and regularly. Mrs Thatcher was so determined never to be late, either in London or at Balmoral, that she was sometimes preposterously early. Once, when she showed up at Buckingham Palace half an hour before the due time, her private secretary got a rap over the knuckles from his counterpart at the Palace.

She found it even more difficult to time her arrival at Balmoral accurately,

given that she usually stayed beforehand with Sir Hector Laing and his wife at their Scottish home on the Findhorn. 'She always left the Laings too soon,' recalled a civil servant, 'so we had to kill time if we were going to get to Balmoral, as expected, for tea.

'Once, after we'd stopped the car way up in the hills, she got out and started tottering up and down the main road in semi-high heels. She was most unsuitably dressed for the Highlands and the locals who passed by gave her some shocked looks when they realized who she was.'

According to her staff, Mrs Thatcher was in considerable awe of the Queen – 'Her curtsey almost reached Australia,' said Lord Powell, one of her principal aides – and the Queen was always the more relaxed of the two. Yet, although Mrs Thatcher seemed under- rather than over-confident when confronted by the monarch, that did not stop the Prime Minister holding forth at considerable length during their weekly audience.

'The Queen found Mrs Thatcher a bit of a frost,' said a former senior courtier. 'Most Prime Ministers go to the Palace or Balmoral to talk over their problems. The Queen then gives them a bit of a boost, partly by encouraging them, partly by offering them a sensible perspective. That was not the way Mrs Thatcher treated her audiences. She came along to tell the Queen what was what. Because of that, the Queen felt she really wasn't much use to her Prime Minister.'

'I did once ask the Queen,' recalled one of her former private secretaries, 'whether an audience with Mrs Thatcher wasn't rather like listening to a public address, much as Gladstone treated Queen Victoria. She indicated that Mrs Thatcher did have her agenda in her reticule and proceeded to go through it without giving the Queen much chance unless she was prepared to interrupt. Well, the Queen is not that sort of person, so audiences tended to be a one-sided rehearsal of what the Prime Minister intended to do.'

'Whether she got a word in edgeways is one of the great untold stories,' agreed a former head of the Foreign Office. 'The Queen had considerable respect for Mrs Thatcher, but always joked that the Prime Minister never listened to a word she said.'

The Queen with Lady Thatcher at the latter's seventieth birthday party, 1995.

There were media stories that the two women had profound and open disagreements about the conduct of the 1984 coal strike and the issue of economic sanctions against South Africa, which Mrs Thatcher opposed and which threatened to split the Commonwealth apart.

One of the Queen's former senior advisers insists that there is no truth in these stories. 'There was a climate to suggest that she was not in sympathy with the way in which Mrs Thatcher was dealing with the coal strike,' he said, 'but that is quite incorrect. She was neither angry nor worried about the way it was handled.'

As far as sanctions against South Africa were concerned, he added, he very much doubted whether the Queen would have said what she thought during the audiences. 'Her sympathies were with the Commonwealth side, she'd got to know and like several black Prime Ministers and it had taken the place of the Empire as the last bit of her inheritance, but I can't remember her putting it on their weekly agenda.

'When the story of their supposed disagreement appeared in the *Sunday Times* in 1986, I was at Windsor with the Queen and told her that Number Ten was in quite a state about it. I suggested that it might be a good idea if she were to ring Mrs Thatcher. She did just that while I was standing at her elbow, and said that the story bore no relation to the facts. The two women commiserated with each other.'

Mrs Thatcher's own aides make it clear how much the Prime Minister tried to take account of the Queen's sensitivities on the Commonwealth. 'She was deeply upset about the sanctions business,' recalled one, 'and I can remember moments when she said, "The Queen wouldn't like that so we can't do it." She said that partly out of respect for the sovereign, partly because it would be very bad news politically if it got around that the Queen disapproved of government policy.'

To the end, the two women remained a mystery to each other. Mrs Thatcher sent the Queen a pair of rubber gloves as a Christmas present after she had seen her washing up at Balmoral without any, but always felt there was something missing in their relationship. The Queen revealed her puzzlement by asking those who knew Mrs Thatcher well all kinds of questions about her.

She asked Lord Runcie, the then Archbishop of Canterbury, whether he regarded Mrs Thatcher as a religious woman, to which he replied, 'I think she is more of a Hebrew than a Christian.' She asked Lord Carrington, 'Do you think Mrs Thatcher will ever change?' He does not say what he replied.

There was clearly a competitive edge between them. Out of sheer weariness, Mrs Thatcher felt compelled to sit down at the annual diplomatic reception in the Palace on two successive years. The Queen, rejoicing in her own apparently limitless stamina, remarked gleefully to Lord Runcie, 'She's keeled over again!'

Harold Wilson, according to one of his private secretaries, attached 'inordinate' significance to his audiences with the Queen and regarded his relationship with her as so important that he even thought of putting off retirement because he felt that she might be in difficulty.

'He'd told the Queen in December 1975 that he intended to resign the following March,' recalls an aide, 'but running through that period were the shenanigans between Princess Margaret and Roddy Llewelyn. Harold told me there were two things which would make him press the hold button on retirement. The first was if there was a disaster in Northern Ireland, the second was if the Queen were to have really serious problems with her sister. "I'm not going to leave her on her own," he said.'

The sad thing was that the Queen eventually became bored with Wilson's boastfulness. 'She thought he was absurd,' Lord Charteris once told me, 'rather like Toad in *Wind in the Willows*.' Wilson was astonished and delighted when the Queen agreed to go to a farewell dinner at Number Ten, to which the entire Labour Cabinet was invited. In her speech afterwards, she said how pleasant it was to come to dinner in the tied cottage at the other end of the Mall. When Wilson had left office, however, she did not want to see much more of him.

'When I was brand-new in my job,' recalled a former courtier, 'I was walking with Wilson in the royal tea-tent at a garden party after he had resigned, and it was obvious that he wanted to get closer to her. I saw by the Queen's expression that she was not giving him the come-hither and then one of my colleagues came up and murmured, "No closer!" She'd had to be frightfully nice to him for all those years and she'd had enough!'

'The thing you have to remember,' explained a civil servant who served three Prime Ministers, 'is that the Queen has reigned for a long time, so none of her Prime Ministers is as special to her as she is to them.'

Her relationship with them has nothing to do with the political party which they lead. According to Martin Charteris, she did not trust Eden and found Ted Heath very heavy weather, partly because of his patent disinterest in the Commonwealth. On the other hand, she felt comfortable enough with Jim

Callaghan to treat him to a spot of feminine charm. On one occasion, according to an aide, 'He was absolutely wowed when she walked with him in the garden at the Palace, picked a lily of the valley and put it in his buttonhole!'

John Major, too, found his audiences with the Queen both hugely enjoyable and helpful. Far from regarding them as a chore, he looked forward to them. It was marvellous, he felt, to share all his hopes and fears with someone who was totally apolitical yet had great experience and wisdom. There was nothing, he felt, that he could not talk to her about, knowing that the only eavesdroppers were the Queen's corgis. He also found that, far from merely listening sympathetically, the Queen often had very pertinent things to say.

There are curiously mixed stories about her relationship with Tony Blair, although, as he told republican friends in Australia, he is a monarchist. One very senior civil servant says that, in Blair's early days in office, he 'neglected the audience, not turning up, it was being squeezed out all the time, and the Palace said it had to have a higher priority.'

The most senior courtiers at the Palace during those years, however, vigorously deny that that was the case, and insist that Blair was punctilious about going to the Palace regularly. 'I can't remember him undoing one Tuesday evening,' said one. One thing at least is clear. As the years have gone by, Blair's audiences with the Queen have tended to become longer and now sometimes last for an hour and a half.

These same former courtiers also defend him against the charge that he tried to hog the limelight at the Queen's Golden Wedding celebrations in 1997 by walking behind the royal couple and shaking hands with people in the crowd. 'Critics ask why Number Ten was involved,' said one. 'Well, we planned the occasion in that way – and asked whether we could stop off in Downing Street for a perfectly simple reason.

'The fact is that there are no convenient loos between Westminster Abbey and the Banqueting Hall, and the Queen and Prince Philip were planning to do what might have been a lengthy walkabout. So, we asked if we could stop off in Number Ten. Then, according to the weather, we could either take a car or walk to the Banqueting Hall. Since it was fine, the

The Queen makes her way to St George's Chapel, Windsor Castle, for the service of the annual Order of the Garter ceremony, June 1999.

Queen said to the Prime Minister, "Why don't we walk?" The idea that it was a Downing Street stitch-up so that he could trail clouds of glory from the Queen is rubbish. It was her idea.'

But does the Queen's influence extend much beyond her Prime Ministerial audiences? Even senior aristocrats whose families have served the Crown for centuries write her off as 'in many ways, merely an ornament' but, if that is true, why are many of the governing class so chary of either crossing or displeasing her?

For one thing, they have a sneaking suspicion that she could somehow affect their careers. 'People in the Establishment,' said an Anglican bishop, 'believe that, if they offend her, she has the power to influence their future – that, if they put a foot wrong, a word will be spoken here or there. Like fearful and ambitious children, they don't want to upset the great mother figure.'

'If you put your foot in it with the Queen,' agreed a former Prime Ministerial private secretary, 'the way it would be transmitted would be via her private secretary. If, for example, an Ambassador made a cock-up of a State visit, it would not go unremarked and the Queen's private secretary is the one who would do the remarking. A State visit can either blight or further an ambassador's career.'

'The fact is,' said David Owen, 'that a lot of people in very important jobs feel they serve the Queen and not the Government, and any Prime Minister knows there is that element in the system. Those people would go the Queen's private secretary if they thought anything was wrong. The Chief of the Defence Staff would not hesitate to talk to her. Not only does the Queen take very seriously the Ambassadors and senior military commanders who leave this country for service overseas, those people very much value their relationship with her.'

Before Sir Christopher Soames and his wife left for Southern Rhodesia in 1979, where he was to be its last Governor, they went to the Palace to take their leave of the Queen. Knowing that Soames had heart problems, the Queen said: 'You do know Salisbury is very high, Christopher, don't you?' Soames replied that he had 'a vet's certificate'. After the Soameses came back to Britain, he was made a Companion of Honour, his wife a Dame of the British Empire. The Queen invested them privately. 'Well, this is nice,' she said. 'I think we thought we might never see each other again!'

The trouble which Downing Street takes to keep the Palace happy suggests that they, too, do not underestimate the Queen's importance. 'We see and talk to Number Ten a lot,' said a recently retired senior courtier, 'and they are very solicitous in ringing us up. "How will this play with the Queen in terms of presentation?" . . . "This is going to be announced, how do you want to address it?"

'Something will come up and we'll say, "We don't think the Queen will wear that." It could be whether X should have a knighthood – if somebody ropey came up, Blair would certainly listen if she spoke – or it could be some overriding issue on which she'd have a very firm, Olympian view based on the wisdom and experience of many years. We usually think of power being exercised in a very public way, but the Queen is a hidden back-stop.'

'She makes it impossible for people to get too far out of line,' agreed a Prime Ministerial private secretary. 'If Blair said, "Let's only have elections every ten years," try telling that to the Queen on a Tuesday night! Can you imagine what would happen to the royal eyebrows? In the final analysis, a Prime Minister has to explain to the Queen what he is doing and, in a case like that, he'd feel like a rat, because she represents moral rectitude in terms of public behaviour and the sanctity of the constitution.'

When it comes to honours, the vast majority come via committees in Downing Street. Only the Order of Merit, the Garter and the Royal Victorian Order are in the gift of the Queen. Yet the suspicion remains among nervous title-hungry wannabes that a royal blackball could still scupper their chances.

'That suspicion gives her considerable power, because both the old and new Establishments care like mad about gongs and appointments,' said a former Tory Cabinet minister. 'Some of them are particularly interested in the OMs, GCVOs and Garters which only she can bestow. Then there are generals who want to be colonels of the great regiments, bishops who covet plum dioceses. A feeling that she may have some say over these appointments gives her enormous influence in massaging the egos of powerful people in this country.'

She seldom in practice seeks to challenge the honours which Prime Ministers propose. 'The Queen is extremely chary of questioning one of the Prime Minister's recommendations,' said a former Cabinet Secretary, 'but the list does go to the Palace in case she has any observations to make. I can remember two occasions when she said, "Are you sure?" In one case, we said,

"We are." In the second, we did it another way.'

Even so, the Palace's scrutiny is by no means cursory. 'When the Wilson resignation honours list was put up in 1976,' said Lord Blake, 'the Queen's secretary, Lord Charteris, made very careful enquiries about some of the people on it, with a view to suggesting that the Queen might veto one or more of them. He told me about it in the bar at White's, a very good place for confidences with everybody drinking like fishes and making a lot of noise.

'He said he'd been in touch with the Inland Revenue to find out whether there had been any jiggery-pokery. In the end, he couldn't find any evidence which suggested that the Queen should not accept the list.'

Everyone, of course, wants to receive their honour from the Queen's own hand. Those who are lucky enough to have several, however, often place more value on those she alone can give. 'My knighthood is the most useful when it comes to business,' said a former Permanent Secretary, 'but the greatest pleasure I felt was in my CVO, partly because it came straight from the Queen and partly because of its comparative rarity.'

'I use my knighthood when I'm working in the Commonwealth,' said another former mandarin, 'but on my personal stationery it's my CVO which I wouldn't want to leave off. It comes personally from the Queen and it's an earnest of her presence and favour.'

That sense of having some sort of relationship with the Queen, of being – however distantly – in touch with the Palace means a great deal to those who enjoy it. They feel themselves to be life members of the Ultimate Club. The Crown is not only the fount of honour but also, as Malcolm Muggeridge believed, the fount of snobbery. It is a Club which has no official membership and only one rule: that those who belong to it should behave entirely honourably and, as a matter of honour, never repeat what the Queen has said. In Washington, it is kiss and tell: in London, bow and hold your tongue.

'Because you've been privileged to speak to the Queen,' said a former Cabinet Secretary, 'it would clearly be a gross breach of courtesy, confidence and loyalty if you were to repeat what she has said to you. All those concerned know that, if they speak out of turn, they will be out of the Ultimate Club.'

'Once you are in that circle,' remarked a former Permanent Secretary, 'you see that preserving the ring of silence which surrounds and protects the Queen is an important part of the mystique of monarchy. You're never told that, you just pick it up. Thereafter, there is always the question in your mind, "Am I approved or am I not?" You've become part of the circle and accepted its norms and you want to continue to be approved of. I wouldn't ever want to do anything to make life more difficult for the Queen.

'In one way, since I left the public service, my membership of the Ultimate Club is no longer of any value to me. I no longer get invitations to garden parties at the Palace but, occasionally, something here in the business might require me to lift the phone to the Queen's private secretary and, partly because of that, I couldn't do other than play the game. It's a continuation of both honour and self-interest. In that way, you remain a member of the Club!'

Invitations to all manner of occasions afford members a sign of the Queen's continuing approval. When they are invited to garden parties, they are shepherded into areas where they at least have a chance of meeting her. They are given pride of place at ceremonial occasions such as the Trooping the Colour. Every November, 1,400 attend the diplomatic reception at the Palace. There are 170 select souls at every State banquet.

Each year, the Queen invites eight or ten even more select souls – senior politicians, ambassadors and other public figures – to a short series of 'dine-and-sleeps' at Windsor. And, for the most favoured, there are invitations to a variety of Royal Family parties.

'Everyone likes to be invited to such occasions,' said a retired courtier whose job it was to draw up the invitation lists, 'because it makes them feel they have a relationship with her. Once you are part of that inner circle, of course, you long for another invitation and, if you don't get one, you feel you've fallen out of favour. You ask yourself, "Where did I go wrong?"'

In his view, the hope that that relationship might continue affects the behaviour of people. 'Those who have been guests of the Queen who are contemplating a bit of a fiddle on their taxes or some other piece of dubious behaviour might easily think, "She's been very nice to me, what would she think of this – and would I ever be invited again?" In that and other ways, she's a civilizing and ameliorating influence on society.'

There are other means by which continuing membership of the Club is conveyed. There are, for example, Christmas cards, not only from the Queen but also from other members of the Royal Family. Proud indeed are those who can sport a full set on their mantelpieces and sideboards. For the ladies, there is that highest mark of intimacy and approval, the royal kiss, sparingly bestowed. Members of the Club care a good deal about such things.

'Yes,' admitted Sonny Ramphal, 'to get no invitations or Christmas cards would certainly hurt. I still get her card, which conveys an intimation of intimacy. I don't think there is an element of snobbery in it, just the quiet satisfaction of being an insider. If you're out of the Club and the card no longer arrives, there would undoubtedly be unquiet dissatisfaction.'

Attendance at ceremonial occasions also helped bind you into the Club, he added. 'Commonwealth leaders have always had a special place at events such as wreath-laying at the Cenotaph and Trooping the Colour. There, they occupy a separate stand with the Prime Minister and Secretary-General. At garden parties, they have their own separate tent.'

They certainly abide by the rule of silence quite as strictly as their British counterparts. 'All the Commonwealth leaders accept that convention,' said Chief Anyaoku, another former Secretary-General. 'No one ever quotes the Queen, not even my own son! When she went to Birmingham University in May 2000, she not only remembered that Emenike was a first-year student but also had him at her right hand for lunch and talked to him for an hour. But he wouldn't tell me what she had said to him!'

As Head of the Commonwealth, the Queen has put up a quite astonishing performance. She has helped to ease it through half a dozen crises which threatened to tear it apart; and, in the process, earned the unqualified love and respect of hundreds of Commonwealth leaders, black, brown and white, republican and Marxist. 'Robert Mugabe may express his venom against the British Government,' said Anyaoku, 'but he would not even begin to associate his anger with the Queen.'

There are all kinds of reasons why the Commonwealth is important to her. It is, as Douglas Hurd says, 'a very vivid part of her inheritance'. It is also an obvious way in which the monarchy can justify its existence in an age where its power and responsibilities at home are so limited. In that sense, the Queen needs the Commonwealth as much as the Commonwealth needs the Queen.

When he first became Secretary-General in 1975, Sonny Ramphal felt it was anachronistic for a monarch to lead the Commonwealth. He soon changed his mind. 'The Queen,' he said, 'transcended the barriers of race, colour and caste very easily, and she was never lofty or remote. In all my fifteen years, I never met a Prime Minister or a president – Marxists and republicans included – who did not set the greatest store by the twenty minutes she spent with each of them at our heads of government meetings.' As Prince Philip once shrewdly remarked, 'She has become the Commonwealth psychotherapist.'

'Even more astonishing,' Ramphal went on, 'I never at any time felt that she behaved in a way aimed at promoting the British national interest. The gender dimension certainly came into it. Because she was a woman, it was easier to believe that she really cared. But', he added drily, 'it had nothing to do with her genetic inheritance!'

'Somehow,' agreed Chief Anyaoku, 'she has been able to transform the position of the monarchy so that it is no longer associated with Britain's colonial past. I cannot believe that her father would have commanded the same sort of respect and admiration.'

Nor is the admiration based only on regal charm. 'She knows more about the Commonwealth than any of her British ministers and most of the Commonwealth ones,' said a former head of the Foreign Office. 'As I found from personal experience, she will ask Commonwealth High Commissioners questions about quite remote things in their countries and, unless they have been very well briefed, they often have no idea what she is talking about.'

'In 1961,' recalled Sir Edward Ford, 'Geoffrey de Freitas, the socialist MP, was appointed High Commissioner in Ghana. He came to the Palace saying, "What's all this about kissing hands? How long is it going to take?" His meeting with the Queen was scheduled for twenty minutes. When he came out thirty-five minutes later, he said, "That's astonishing! I've found out more about Ghana in the last half-hour than I have in three weeks going round Whitehall."'

In a curious way, the Queen always seems happier, more relaxed, more at home on Commonwealth visits than she does on public occasions in Britain. The stiffness and the reserve vanish, the sense of burden falls away; and she responds to the spontaneous outpouring of joy with which she is usually greeted. The late Kenneth Kaunda of Zambia simply called her Elizabeth. For the Queen, the Commonwealth is a time for fun as well as duty. It is her overseas version of the horse and the dog.

'The banquet which she hosts at heads of government meetings,' recalled Admiral Robert Woodard, 'is more like a family dinner party. It's filled with

merriment and leg-pulling. When she gets up to speak, they'll roar with laughter and heckle her. "Come on, Your Majesty," they'll shout, "do you really mean that?" And she'll say, "Do be quiet for a minute! I'm trying to make a speech!" They really are joyous occasions.'

Once beyond these shores, she also cares less for the niceties of formally correct behaviour. When she greeted the wives of Australia's political leaders in Sydney in 2000, her smile was just as broad for those who did not curtsey as for those who did.

These days, it would take bloody revolution to deter her from making a scheduled Commonwealth visit. In 1971, on Alec Douglas-Home's advice, she did not go to the heads of government meeting in Singapore because the Foreign Office were afraid that there was going to be a bust-up about the issue of arms to South Africa. She was reluctant to accept the advice at the time and vowed that she would never accept such advice again. In March 1995, the Foreign Office again advised her to delay a visit to South Africa until the security situation improved. 'She replied, "Certainly not,"' said Admiral Woodard. ' "They need me as quickly as I can get down there!"'

By that time, the Queen had already built a close personal relationship with Nelson Mandela. 'It began at the 1991 heads of government meeting in Harare,' recalled Anyaoku. 'Mandela had been invited to Salisbury by Robert Mugabe with my agreement although, at that time, he was only the leader of the ANC and not a head of government. Indeed, South Africa was not even a member of the Commonwealth. I was one of the first to arrive and was surprised to see Mandela talking to the Zimbabwe liaison officer. There had been some misunderstanding, and he was obviously expecting to come to the Queen's banquet, which is strictly for heads of government.

'So Robert Fellowes and myself had to decide what advice to give the Queen, who at that point had not even met Mandela. When we told her what the situation was, she immediately said, "Let's have him." She had absolutely no hesitation. I thought it was a remarkable piece of judgement. After all, Mrs Thatcher had called Mandela a terrorist at our Vancouver meeting in 1987. So he came to the banquet, in May 1994 he became President of South Africa and, in the following month, South Africa rejoined the Commonwealth.'

The Queen meeting President Nyere of Tanzania at a Commonwealth conference, 1979.

That was the beginning of a remarkable friendship. When Mandela came to London for a State visit in 1996, he poured out his admiration for 'this gracious lady' at a lunch he gave for her. 'In reply,' said a former mandarin who was there, 'she got up without a note in her hand and praised "this wonderful man".'

Mandela had said that he would prefer a party at the Albert Hall with thousands of young people present rather than a State banquet at Buckingham Palace, and the Queen readily agreed. 'She came and sat with him in his box,' recalled the former mandarin, 'and, when Mandela stood up and did his famous bop as Phil Collins's band was belting it out, the Queen stood up and did the same. I was hosting a box four away from theirs and one of the more establishment figures with me said, "Good heavens, the Queen is dancing!"' That is the effect the Commonwealth has on her. It is also one episode among many which reveals just how remarkable a Queen she is.

How ought one to judge her half-century on the throne? Predictably, she has plenty of critics, some of them former senior courtiers. They charge her with being dull, staid, far too dilatory in slimming down the monarchy and utterly lacking in both initiative and imagination. The result, they claim, is that the monarchy now seems irrelevant to many people.

The other side of the coin, say the Queen's admirers, is that her long reign has been astonishingly error-free. 'You can count the blunders she has made on one hand,' said Lord Rees-Mogg, 'and it hardly comes to one a decade.'

She entirely failed to recognize the scale of the public reaction to Princess Diana's death and, as a result, pitched the monarchy into a mini-crisis; was widely criticized in the Tory Party for taking Harold Macmillan's advice to send for Alec Douglas-Home without consulting more widely; and her decision to allow Sir Anthony Blunt, her Surveyor of Pictures, to remain a member of the royal household after he had been unmasked as a KGB agent is still regarded by some courtiers as an astonishing lapse of judgement.

It is easy for critics to sniff that, while she has very rarely put a foot wrong, she has also not put one very far forward; that she failed to give her children much sense of maternal warmth; that she has remained a woman of routine and convention. The standing of the monarchy is plainly lower than when she came to the throne and, no doubt, she is partly responsible. The behaviour of her children and changing times are equally to blame.

When all that is said, however, she has undoubtedly been one of the most admirable monarchs in British history. She is absolutely straight, extremely shrewd, utterly dedicated and has led a blameless life. As one of her private secretaries put it, 'She is pure gold.'

She has been a faithful and abiding presence through one of the most difficult periods in our history; and since, as Lord Charteris once remarked, 'she is as strong as a yak', she is likely to be on the throne for some time to come. She has no intention of abdicating and could even become the longest-reigning monarch in our history.

'Queen Elizabeth the Second will be a hard act to follow'

10 The Modern Monarchy

It is a truism to say that, despite the sterling character of the Queen, the grandest days of the British monarchy are long past. The aristocratic hierarchy over which it once towered is being rapidly sidelined and enfeebled. The hereditary principle, of which the monarchy is the ultimate expression, is being rubbished by a Prime Minister who, ironically, reckons to be a monarchist. The Crown is now perched on top of a crumbling ruin, dependent entirely on the goodwill of the public and their fickle political masters. For the monarchy, sadly, there are infinitely less grand days ahead.

The lurking question, indeed, is no longer what kind of future it has, but whether it has a future at all.

There was a time, but three-quarters of a century ago, when its grandeur still held a sense of mystery and magic for an instinctively deferential if not subservient people. The very haughtiness of the Royal Family conveyed a feeling of impregnable self-importance. They behaved as if they scarcely needed public approval to justify their existence. They wielded their influence over society with a certainty that it was they, and they alone, who set its tone.

The fact that our present Queen is a paragon of good behaviour – with a diffidence and modesty absent in almost all her predecessors – only serves to disguise the truth that our monarchy is now hopelessly out of kilter with the modern world in both size and style. Its gallimaufry of bizarre and archaic titles – Mistress of the Robes, Woman of the Bedchamber, Page of the Presence, Silver-Stick-in-Waiting – suggests a period drama on television rather than a modern institution. Its vast agglomeration of property – half-a-dozen palaces, hundreds of grace-and-favour residences, a battalion of servants – also belongs less to the needs of a modern head of state, however elevated, than to a past age of power.

The scale of the Windsors' lifestyle is often farcically inflated. Even a minor royal such as Prince Edward inhabits a vast pile totally out of proportion to his public value or significance. Others of the Queen's offspring can sometimes behave with an hauteur which is both deeply unattractive and utterly out of place.

Yet, behind the grandiose façade, senior courtiers have a keen sense that, while royal stories may sell newspapers, the position and popularity of the monarchy hang by gossamer threads. They have expended a great deal of mental energy wondering how best to slim it down, make it more cost-effective and user-friendly. Nothing is more indicative of their nervous sense of rapidly changing times than the way in which many of them cling to the life-raft of that magnificently performed ceremonial which is both the monarchy's shop-window and its sole remaining public glory.

'I think ceremony is at the heart of it,' said one long-serving royal servant. 'That is the thing which makes the monarch different and special. If the State Opening of Parliament were scaled down, it would be a terrible retreat. If you took that away, other ceremonial might crumble and then the monarchy itself might crumble with it. Once you lose the ceremonial, what's the point of the sovereign?'

Perhaps that is one reason why the Queen herself pays such meticulous attention to the tiniest detail of the monarchy's public performances. 'At the post-mortem after a parade,' recalled a former senior courtier, 'she would say, "That man in the back rank, third from the right, kept moving his fingers on his rifle. Why did he do that? Is he mad?"'

A guard commander at Windsor Castle was given a message by the Queen's footman that she had noticed that one of his men on duty in the quadrangle was standing three feet to the left of where he should be. An admiral commanding the Royal Yacht was told by the Queen to inform the new director of music that he was taking up his position at the wrong moment during the Beating the Retreat ceremony. When, six months later, the director performed the manoeuvre at precisely the *right* moment, the Queen turned and gave the admiral an approving nod. He was amazed that she had remembered such a minor detail.

If such minutiae demand her personal scrutiny the Queen, too, evidently has a strong sense of the monarchy's fragility. The Windsors' family life may be the very opposite of well-drilled, but it can at least display excellence in its flawless management of public occasions.

Since the death of Princess Diana, the Queen has done her very best, given her age and character, to modify her style in accordance with the mores of an age utterly different from the one in which she arrived on the throne. She is almost infinitely biddable. If her advisers tell her to sign footballs, she signs. If they tell her to sit on moquette settees and chat to the inhabitants of council flats, she chats as best she may. If they ask her to bowl up to a McDonald's in her Bentley, she bowls – though she does not eat. Victoria commanded, Elizabeth obeys.

The whole thing makes Prince Charles spit – 'Why do they ask Mummy to do those ridiculous things which just aren't her?' he grizzles – but it is working in a modest fashion.

The organizers of a recent visit to an Oxford college were startled by the new angle of attack. 'We had a plan,' said one, 'which included a church service, an exhibition of the college's history, a garden party and lunch in hall. The Palace said, "Good," but insisted that there must be walkabouts, lots of the Queen meeting students all dressed according to their activities – sportsmen and women in sports gear, actors in acting garb – all with plenty of photo opportunities. We were told that the church service mustn't last a minute longer than half an hour, she mustn't spend more than ten minutes in the exhibition, including another photo opportunity – and she must do something for the town. So we arranged for her to watch some Asian children dancing. It was a great success, but the whole direction of the visit struck me as blatantly if not vulgarly populist.'

In private, of course, the Queen wants nothing to do with this necessary if, as some might think, demeaning nonsense. At nine every morning in Buckingham Palace, her personal piper plays her favourite speys and reels as she finishes her modest breakfast. At Balmoral, guests are warned that they must on no account sit on Queen Victoria's chair; and Australian Governors-General of proletarian origin are astonished to be asked by a footman not merely whether they would like to have a bath run for them but whether they would also like to have their back scrubbed.

Given his love of tradition, Prince Charles would wholly approve of back-scrubbing. What makes him fume with rage and frustration is that, as he sees it, his parents are putting his inheritance at risk by failing to set in train the reforms which the monarchy urgently needs.

It is not merely that, in his view, they have neither the taste nor the style with which he believes himself to be abundantly endowed. It is also, at a much deeper level, that he hates what his aides call 'the clever-dick modernism' which attempts to give his mother an image makeover; and that any suggestions he makes for slimming down and reshaping the monarchy are blocked by a father who shouts at him and a mother who says nothing.

'He gets very upset about meetings of the Way Ahead group, which is supposed to be the forum where the monarchy discusses its future,' said an aide. 'He finds the idea of the Queen being executive chairman of that meeting utterly bizarre because that isn't the sort of thing she does and, if anybody disagrees with what the Duke of Edinburgh thinks, they are shouted down. He regards his father as a bully and feels that his mother simply lets her husband be dominant and get what he wants.

'He's also annoyed that he's there on the same level as his brothers and sister, yet he is the heir and they are not. There's Edward – Mr Know-it-all, and who cares what he thinks – Andrew who only wants to talk about trains and transport, and Anne who thinks the whole thing is ridiculous anyway. The Prince of Wales is convinced there is never going to be a proper discussion about the future of the monarchy in that setting.

'He also feels his mother doesn't really understand how things are because she has never been out there, never been a normal human being, didn't go to school, never mixed with real people, never suffered the

The Queen in Milan on her State visit to Italy, October 2000.

indignities which real people have to deal with all the time – and which the younger end of the family have to cope with too.'

While courtiers at both St James's and Buckingham Palace remark that they have seldom met anyone who has as little real confidence as Prince Charles, he does have some very clear ideas about how he would set about reshaping the monarchy. Whether those ideas are anything like radical enough remains to be seen.

'He has it all worked out how he would be King,' said one of his aides, 'though he doesn't talk about it even with those of us who are closest to him. But he'd clearly have to have a look at the family assets – Kensington Palace, Buckingham Palace, St James's, Clarence House, Holyrood – and he'd have to ask the question, "Just how many of those can you afford?" because the accountants who now rule the world here will make him ask it.' Charles, indeed, now has an accountant, in the shape of Michael Peat, as his private secretary.

As for wider questions like the Commonwealth and the Crown's role within it, 'He finds it hard to see how that can be kept going for a long time. There are too many other places to go to – Europe, for example, which everyone says is important.'

As for the other issue which bears on the monarchy's immediate future, Camilla and whether he should marry her, clerics close to Charles have the sense that, for the moment, he is resigned to leaving things where they are. If not cock-a-hoop, both he and his aides feel that the tide has turned and is now running strongly in his favour.

'There might have been a time,' said an aide, 'when we traded on approval from over the road (i.e. Buckingham Palace) to advance the position with Camilla, but it is now sufficiently solid and developed that we don't need to feel they are on our side. We are convinced that the bulk of informed public opinion is. The Prince of Wales's view is that this is how it is and, if Mummy doesn't like it, too bad. He has decided to stop being angry and annoyed that she doesn't approve.

'Where we are now is that they can have everything they want apart from marriage, but, if you ask, how could we structure that so it doesn't mean Queen Camilla, I don't believe that arranging a morganatic marriage (by which Camilla would have no right to Charles's titles or property) is all that difficult.

It needs an Order in Council but, providing you have the Prime Minister on your side, that can be fixed. You can fix anything.'

A good many senior courtiers and former courtiers are convinced that Charles and Camilla will marry, and within the foreseeable future, given that the Queen does not withhold her approval. Sir Michael Peat would certainly never have become Charles's private secretary unless he were a convinced Camilla man. All kinds of people to whom I have talked speak warmly of her.

'She's a patient woman,' said someone who has been a regular visitor to both Highgrove and Camilla's own home, 'unthreatening and totally uninterested in power. She's also cool – which enables her to cope with his pouting and his obsession with his media image – she has the easy social poise of her class and she gets on splendidly with William and Harry.'

For the moment, however, everything – including the nature of his relationship with Camilla – is on hold so far as Prince Charles is concerned. He has been waiting in the starting blocks with mounting impatience for a very long time and wonders what the situation will be by the time he has a chance to put his ideas into practice.

'He feels the monarchy will go one of two ways,' said one of his aides. 'One, the desire on the part of youth to destroy all the old institutions and reinvent everything will mean that the monarchy will be swept away with it. Two, people will get fed up with all that, see that it is not producing a benefit for the country and come back to regarding the monarchy as part of stability. His job is to make sure it is the latter, but all he can do is hope and do his best.

'The Queen may reign for another twenty years and he has to get his time of waiting right, taking on more State functions without actually having the top job, and keep Prince William sorted.' After a period when those who know him say that William wanted nothing to do with becoming heir to the throne – 'Look what it has done to my family,' he used to remark – he is, according to his father's aides, 'warming to the idea so long as it isn't for a long time yet'.

For the next few years at least, it will be extremely hard to perceive just what kind of man William is through the fog of spin and relentless media fabrication. For the moment, opinions of him from those who have seen something of him are a trifle mixed. Charles's aides think that William is more impressive than

his father at the same age. A recently retired courtier, on the other hand, judged that 'he has something of his mother's troubled quality'.

If Prince Philip should predecease the Queen, there would be a huge shift of power within the Royal Family. Charles would become the unchallenged prime mover, and the rift between St James's and Buckingham Palace would stand a real chance of being healed. We would then see whether Charles's ideas for reshaping the monarchy go far enough in reducing its present over-inflated scale or whether he cherishes a grandiose vision of its future in line with his grandmother's instincts. At least he now has, in Michael Peat, a practised axe-man at his side.

If and when Charles succeeds his mother on the throne, we shall also see whether he will be the sort of King who can give the monarchy a chance of long-term survival. In many ways, his style is well suited to the modern age. He is excellent at dealing with ordinary people, both face to face and in the mass. He has concerns which are not only fashionable but also worthwhile. He can laugh at himself and has a self-evident vulnerability which sits well with our touchy-feely world. In all those ways, he seems more like one of us than the present Queen.

On the other hand, if his track record is anything to go by, he will seek to be more interventionist in areas of public policy than his mother ever was. Politicians and civil servants may well find that thoroughly irritating. Tuesday evening audiences at the Palace, if they continued, would certainly be of an entirely different quality. Charles is also unlikely to be as efficient and focused as his mother. 'He works for a week and then needs three weeks off,' as someone who knows him well remarked recently. Civil servants who have dealt with him say that there is something of the gadfly about him, that he is apt to flip from one issue to the next, that there is a shallow quality about both his mind and some of his enthusiasms.

Sceptics, though, will ask what, in any case, will be the point of the monarchy in the years ahead? They might concede that it will at least be valuable in terms of tourist revenue, and as a high-class soap opera for those who like such things. The Queen Mother's funeral, however, made it perfectly clear that, to very large numbers of the public, it means a great deal more

Queen Elizabeth with Prince Charles and Prince William at the Braemar Games, September 2001.

than that. A fringe institution would surely never attract such evident love and such profound appreciation.

Monarchy has a great many virtues, hard though republicans find it to acknowledge them. For one thing, it rules out competition for the top job of head of state, and spares us the likely alternative – some pompous, status-grubbing ex-politician. When admirably fulfilled, as it has been over these last decades, it perfectly embodies the ideal of un-self-interested duty and service, unfashionable qualities but without which any society is much the poorer. In the case of Britain, it carries the force of tradition as an embodiment of the national identity. It also adds to the gaiety of nations. It would add even more if the obvious rift within the Royal Family could be healed. Then the cross-fire between the palaces could end; and the spin doctors be honourably retired. The Queen's unexpected public support for Charles in his handling of Prince Harry's drinking and drug-taking was an inspired step in the right direction.

The British people are not fools and, even if the young among us seldom think about the monarchy and what it does, they may well baulk at the prospect of an infinitely more boring and less splendid alternative to the Windsors. If, in the years ahead, we all come to the conclusion that a monarchy is what we still want, then the present Queen, with all her dignity and steadfastness, will have played a major part in that decision.

Prince Charles may think he will do the job better than his mother, entertain more splendidly, reach out more effectively to his people. He should not, however, delude himself. Queen Elizabeth II, for all her faults, will be a hard act to follow.

Index

Picture Acknowledgements

Page viii: copyright Rex Features/Dave Hartley.
Page 4: copyright PA/John Stillwell.
Page 8: copyright Camera Press/Spice.
Pages 12, 16, 24 & 28: copyright Hulton Getty.
Page 36: copyright AP.
Page 42: copyright PA.
Pages 48 & 52: copyright Camera Press.
Page 56: copyright PA.
Page 60: copyright Corbis.
Page 68: copyright Camera Press/Godfrey Argent.
Page 72: copyright Camera Press/Patrick Lichfield.
Page 76: copyright David Montgomery.
Page 80: copyright Tim Graham.
Page 88: copyright Hulton Getty.
Page 96: copyright Daily Telegraph/Anthony Marshall.
Page 100: copyright Ben Curtis/PA Photos.
Page 108: copyright Camera Press/SUS.
Page 116: copyright PA.
Page 124: copyright Reginald Davis.
Page 128: copyright Hulton Getty.
Page 140: copyright Camera Press/Lord Snowdon.
Page 152 : copyright Camera Press/David Secombe.
Page 164: copyright News International Syndication/Peter Nicholls.
Page 168: copyright Popperfoto/Stephen Hird.
Page 176: copyright PA.
Page 180: copyright Express Syndication/Reg Lancaster.
Page 184: copyright PA/John Stillwell.
Page 192: copyright Camera Press/Peter Griffiths.
Page 200: copyright Ian Jones.
Page 204: copyright PA/Ben Curtis.